THE
CONSCIOUS
PROFESSIONAL

Appreciating your leadership!

May you find some tools in here to help you along the way.

Lead on!

Jessica

THE
CONSCIOUS
PROFESSIONAL

Transform
Your Life
at Work

Jessica Hartung
FOUNDER OF Integrated Work

TREELIGHT PRODUCTIONS
BOULDER, COLORADO

Published by Treelight Productions, LLC
5408 Idylwild Trail, Suite A
Boulder, Colorado 80301

Manuscript prepared with the help and guidance of Rick and Melissa Killian, Killian Creative, Boulder, Colorado. www.killiancreative.com

Illustrations on pages 16 and 17 by Ron Ruelle. All rights reserved. www.ronruelle.com

Design by Peter Gloege, LOOK Design Studio.

To protect privacy, the names and identifying details have been changed in stories and illustrations. In others, various clients facing similar challenges or circumstances have been melded into one with different names, etc. Stories and illustrations in the book have been given strictly as examples to represent circumstances as they tend to play out using the principles and practices we advocate. Every situation is unique, however, and I acknowledge that events may play out differently as you apply them. The point is to keep learning and improving using the content here as guidelines, not strict prescriptions to every situation.

Library of Congress Control Number: 2018913373

ISBN: 978-1-7328075-0-1 (paperback)
ISBN: 978-1-7328075-1-8 (hard cover)
ISBN: 978-1-7328075-2-5 (Kindle)
ISBN: 978-1-7328075-3-2 (ePub)

Printed in the United States of America
27 26 25 24 23 22 21 20 19 (KDP) 1 2 3 4 5 6 7 8 9 10

TABLE OF CONTENTS

PART FOUR: THE SKILL SHIFTS

This book is dedicated to

EVERYDAY CHANGE MAKERS

growing the mindsets
and skillsets necessary
to make positive shifts
in their communities.

And

To the staff, clients, and partners
of Integrated Work.
Thank you for charting
new territory as
conscious professionals.

What people have the capacity to choose,
they have the ability to change.

—MADELEINE K. ALBRIGHT
former US Secretary of State
and US Ambassador to the United Nations

To love what you do
and feel like it matters,
how could anything
be more fun?

—KATHARINE GRAHAM
First American Female Fortune 500 CEO

Success is liking yourself,
liking what you do,
and liking how you do it.

—MAYA ANGELOU

INTRODUCTION:
SHIFTS MATTER

The strongest principle of growth
lies in human choice.

—MARY ANNE EVANS
author of *Middlemarch*, *Silas Marner*,
and other classics*

WHEN LEAH WAS PROMOTED to her first management posi-tion within the agency, she was ecstatic. She loved what they did—ensuring quality preventive care for children all across America—and this new position would give her a stronger voice in that mission. Her vision of really making a difference seemed closer than ever.

But Leah had no idea of the amount of bureaucracy and the roadblocks she would need to navigate as a manager, even to get simple things done. Soon, her enthusiasm faded. Moreover, her inability to get things done well made her miserable. Without realizing it, she was passing her misery on to her staff.

Rather than building new momentum, each meeting she led seemed to leave her team members more disconnected from each

---

* Mary Anne Evans (1819–1880) wrote under the male pen name George Eliot to ensure that her works would be taken seriously. They were.

other and their mission. For months, the drama and trauma of restructuring, new performance measures, and compliance issues dominated the conversation. Little time and attention were devoted to helping kids get the services they needed, let alone making it easier for more of them to do so. The attention was on internal agency problems, not solving problems for the people they were supposed to be serving. Leah was growing frustrated and discouraged, and those emotions were starting to seep into everything she did.

Disappointment wasn't what she'd expected out of her career. She was being well paid, and she loved her job, but she wasn't happy with who she was becoming as she stepped up the ladder. How could that be? How could she work so hard for something, get it, and then regret what it was doing to her?

I met with Leah on a sunny afternoon for our initial coaching session. In contrast to the weather outside, her office felt chilly. We talked. We pictured what her world would be like if things were the way she'd imagined—making powerful strides forward to help ensure quality preventive care to kids who need it and handling the various roadblocks and leadership challenges with ease. What would her day-to-day operations feel like? How would it look from inside her division? From the outside? How would she feel? How would she conduct herself? How would her people perceive things? What benefits and changes would her team experience? After painting a coherent picture, we began figuring out how to move closer to that vision.

With no money in her budget for workshops or individual coaching for her team members, Leah knew she needed to pull herself and her team up by their own bootstraps if things were going to get better. Their training ground would have to be the day-to-day affairs of her department.

Leah and I began to look at specific issues and regularly scheduled events—staff problems she was facing, upcoming meetings, issues she needed to address, presentations to her peers, the one-on-one sessions with her team members, etc.—to identify focal points and strategies for being more inspirational and effective. Aware that she needed to make changes, she quickly became motivated to develop her new outlook and the corresponding skills she needed to run things differently.

She reminded herself to connect with and lead from her values, driven by her team's potential to make a difference. She needed to bring more of her best self into her work. Shifting her sense of who she was from a "bureaucrat with no control" to an inspiring force for good—the "captain of her own destiny" on a mission to touch lives—gave her a renewed spirit of engagement. Where the walls seemed to be closing in on her before, she now saw possibilities.

Her new outlook and skill development—better facilitation of meetings, improved communication and active listening, understanding each team member's place in relationship to the others, etc.—equipped her to leverage each interaction to energize her team toward innovation, improvement, and greater cohesion. She practiced reframing issues and seeing them from the multiple perspectives of her team members, their higher-ups, and their stakeholders. We practiced building a positive future in her mind, to help her see opportunities in the events she experienced daily. Always looking for new ways to advance the mission, she became known for making thoughtful, strategic connections among team members and helping them share expertise across different departments.

Leah's personal growth agenda became linked to fulfilling the mission of the organization, to her values, and to her reason for being on the planet. Over the next eight months, the morale and productivity of her division significantly improved. She felt more connected to those on her team and much more positive and engaged in her work. Their measures of impact were trending upward. The change was dramatic. She became a driving force for the team and for organizational growth, and she *liked* who she was being at work.

Years later, Leah still refers to that time as a pivot point in developing her ability to lead. She has now advanced to the highest levels of civilian leadership and has her choice of opportunities. Her deliberate personal growth has had a tremendously positive ripple effect throughout her agency and the programs they administer. Getting to know other leaders who use similar methods to inspire themselves and their teams has also been a professional highlight for Leah. She has made several new professional friendships with colleagues in other agencies, and when they get together to share ideas and analyze current events, she always learns something new. Not only that, but she says her career is now *fun*—and her approach to learning and making change has also made a huge difference in her family relationships and in her volunteer work with her kids' school. She's having the time of her life because of the personal sense of meaning she gets from solving real challenges in the world and using skills she built on the job.

What was the difference? Leah discovered the power of choice, and the path toward what I like to call the "Third Paycheck."

What was the difference? Leah discovered the power of choice, and the path toward what I like to call the *Third Paycheck.*

Building Your Personal, Portable Capital

When we get a job, it comes with a paycheck—we trade our time, talent, and focus for financial compensation. That's a great thing, of course, because it makes so many other things in our lives possible—like buying food, having a place to live, and purchasing things or experiences that give us joy. That is the power of the *First Paycheck.*

However, most of us long for a sense of impact and challenge beyond just financial gain. It's not just about money; it's about enjoying our lives! There's an emotional reward when the organization you work for has a positive purpose. You feel good about your contribution to the company. And usually you feel good about your co-workers too, as Leah did when her new approach to work created a more enjoyable workplace. Emotional reward is what I consider the *Second Paycheck,* and the methods in this book will help you increase your Second Paycheck significantly. A lot of people are willing to trade in a little (and sometimes a lot) of the First Paycheck if they can get more of the Second. Truth is, when we create emotional satisfaction with our work, we are better able to pursue First Paycheck results with joy.

But there is important compensation beyond being satisfied with our work experience. What paycheck exists beyond financial and emotional rewards? The skills and personal growth we build on the job—which we will carry with us for the rest of our lives. The *Third Paycheck* represents the personal and professional development our jobs can bring us. We choose to develop on the job so we can do more, be more, and impact the causes we care about beyond our profession.

Change makers who long to see positive change in the world, in their communities and families—those who want to make a bigger difference in a wider sphere—feel a pull to develop the skills needed to accomplish their vision. They need the mindsets, wisdom, and skills to match their passion for change. That's why the Third Paycheck rewards of personal and professional development matter so much. Growing transferable skills builds your personal, portable capital, as well as the capacity to do what you want to do.

More specifically, the Third Paycheck includes insights, perspective changes, work experience, and new skills. These things improve our ability to solve increasingly complex and difficult challenges. This paycheck represents the increased capacity that comes from stretching ourselves to become more competent and confident leaders (regardless of job titles). It comes as a result of growing ourselves and our careers so we are not only better at our jobs, but we also become better human beings. All while getting the work done.

Self-directed, on-the-job growth is up to you. You can take the "muck" of work and use it as a learning laboratory, designed just for you, running experiments that build your skills and increase your capacity to handle complexity and higher-level challenges. A Third Paycheck is something we create for ourselves through our choices. No one else in your company needs to know or care about your choice to learn and grow from whatever comes your way. You don't need to ask permission, wait for the right opportunity, or get a new job in order to start learning. This book will help you frame your current work so you can grow right where you are.

Seeing work through the lens of development and learning changes the meaning of what happens on the job. Challenges start to become puzzles to solve, and experimenting with new approaches becomes exciting. After just six months or so, you can look back and see tremendous transformation, not just in your job but in *yourself.* You realize the value of taking time out to reflect on what truly matters. As you explore the next (and slightly terrifying) stretch beyond your comfort zone, you will find that you are willing to keep moving forward because you are learning how you can benefit yourself, the people you care about, and your mission.

This book will help you frame your current work so you can grow right where you are.

People who care about making this kind of impact—and want to increase it throughout their careers—are those most interested in earning the Third Paycheck. They are purpose-driven, personally and professionally. These are people I like to call "conscious professionals." Why? Because they take responsibility for their experience and increase their self-awareness and self-mastery *through their work.*

Want even more good news? Earning the Third Paycheck tends to have a profound, positive effect on the First and Second Paychecks as well.

When competence is combined with conviction, mountains move. The point of individual development is to grow the positive impact within ourselves so we can spread solutions, compassion, and new ideas to our communities. Being a conscious professional means choosing to get better at what we do and who we are, *deliberately.*

Leverage This Book for Your Third Paycheck

Rather than just writing a book about how other people have grown, I wrote this book to help you use your current workplace to grow your capacity to achieve your personal mission—regardless of job title. I want to help you create a Third Paycheck for yourself and those you impact. I want to accelerate your development of personal portable capital—the skills, abilities, and capacities that will take you to the next level of your career, even if it's at a different organization, or in a different field.

*Being a conscious professional means choosing to get better at what we do and who we are, **deliberately**.*

Each chapter is designed to apply to everyday circumstances and challenges. You will learn how you can influence things for the better, even if you are not the one in charge. Each chapter is also introduced with a "shift": a practical transformation that grows your Third Paycheck. These shifts are based on common challenges, matched with methods I have tested time and again with professionals in business, nonprofits, government agencies, and organizations of all kinds, including my firm. Each shift describes the mindset change I hope you get from reading that chapter. These shifts represent the little attitude adjustments and micro-identity shifts that change work from simply accomplishing tasks into a place to flourish. I can tell you honestly, *they work*.

At the same time, no one knows your organization or context like you do. Please take the ideas and stories here as fodder for creating approaches to practice your skills and develop your imagination to picture a better future, whatever situation you're in.

Because I have found that reflection is the Miracle-Gro® of professional development, each chapter ends with a handful of questions that you can use and reuse to bring these shifts into your work life. Having space to record thoughts and insights lets you keep track of your Third Paychecks in a simple but clear way.

(This is why I also suggest you always keep a journal close by as you read, or another mechanism for recording your insights—but we'll talk more about that in Chapter Five.)

At the end of each chapter, I have included a list of benefits for doing the reflection exercises to make clear what you are investing time to create. Readers who do the reflection exercises from the beginning are more likely to follow through to real change. You may also develop your own reflection questions that call forth big insights for you. (You'll find additional resources, worksheets, and opportunities for support at www.consciousprofessional.com.)

Because changing your thinking changes your experience, time spent in reflection puts you in the driver's seat of your career. It allows you to define success on your own terms and lead from your values. Reflection exercises activate and integrate your perspective on how each shift might best serve you. Your experience, ideas, hopes, and concerns are essential to creating fulfilling, meaningful work.

As you make conscious choices to integrate what you've learned, you'll grow. No one can do that for you, but it sure helps to have some support! The concepts and practices in this book are designed to help you take the first steps on a career-long—and lifelong—path of getting more out of what you do every day and developing who you become in the process.

It is time to stop waiting for someone to save us.

It is time to face the truth of our situation—that we're all in this together, that we all have a voice—and figure out how to mobilize the hearts and minds of everyone in our workplaces and communities.

—MARGARET WHEATLEY
author of *Leadership and the New Science*

PART ONE

THE CALL TO CHANGE

GROWING IN PLACE changes how we perceive

work. Our experience is different when we use our effort

to develop ourselves. Conscious professionals bring their

values to their work, striving for greater positive impact

in the world by developing the mindsets and skillsets that

benefit their lives. This approach will transform your life

at work because it changes the purpose of work.

THE SHIFT:

—FROM—

"Work is my J-O-B"

—TOWARD—

"Work is where
I practice being the hero
of my own story."

LEARNING YOUR
WAY FORWARD

To achieve greatness, start where you are,
use what you have, do what you can.

—ARTHUR ASHE
three-time Grand Slam winner,
social activist, and conscious leader[1]

AS A JUNIOR at the University of Michigan, I got a part-time telemarketing position. I had never worked in an office environment before. My previous jobs had been in food service, childcare, or retail. Now I made sales calls to find out what type of mainframe and minicomputers a business had, and whether they would be willing to set an appointment to learn about the software we sold that increased the efficiency of collaboration on documents edited by multiple people—sort of a pre-internet era Google Docs that ran on PCs connected via modems. Making cold calls like that was a new experience, as was the technology. From the beginning, I knew I had a lot to learn.

A few months after I started, the boss of our small team left. They didn't hire anyone to fill his position, and the team and I continued working as we had before. I occasionally asked the managers above me for direction and help, but the answers I got from them were far from useful. They didn't seem to understand running a telemarketing group any more than I did. I was amazed.

I decided that if they didn't know, maybe I should find out for myself.

That decision changed my life.

It was a little like solving a mystery or working on a puzzle. I talked to friends and relatives about what I was working on and whether they knew how people dealt with the issues our company faced. I researched how to establish telemarketing departments. I read books about phone sales, talked to the manager of another call center, and then started implementing what I'd learned. I grew my abilities and myself by rising to the occasion—by filling the "holes" in my own knowledge and the "gaps" between what we collectively knew as a team and what we needed to know to get better at what we did. My colleagues weren't as interested in researching, but they were happy to try out whatever I was having success with.

It wasn't too long before we got better. Our appointment rates were higher, we were making more calls per day, and we had more team spirit. These improvements got noticed. Eventually, I was asked to manage the group, even though others were older and more experienced than I was. I was just having fun, trying to learn how to be better—and suddenly I was getting promoted for it!

The secret ingredient that made work better wasn't outside of me; it was inside. It was a drive toward curiosity about finding a better way to meet needs. And then letting that curiosity lead me to initiate new things. The work relationships with my teammates improved when we felt connected to doing something that mattered. At this part-time job, which I took just to occupy my time on my way to another career, I experienced the intersection of clarity of purpose and a drive to grow, before I even had the words to express the concepts.

I never saw work the same way again. Whenever I started a new position, I learned I couldn't expect those at higher levels to know what I needed to do to be successful—nor provide me the training necessary to grow into a better employee, let alone take an interest in my professional goals and ambitions. In my first office work experience, I realized if I wanted to be a more competent employee and become good at what I did, I was on my own to do it, with no budget to buy resources or hire consultants. I had to learn to "grow in place."

I was just having fun, trying to learn how to be better—and suddenly I was getting promoted for it!

Neither the lack of resources nor a budget really mattered. I had opportunities to learn all around me. What I needed to do was identify them and come up with a plan for filling the gaps in a way that kept me connected to the relevant team of people and our business goals. I didn't need someone else's permission. In fact, my supervisors rewarded me for tactfully taking initiative. I learned I could not only trust my instincts and invest myself in figuring out how to make improvements, but that it was actually a good thing to do. This made my work more enjoyable and meaningful. (Today, this is called employee engagement.)

It became difficult to see a downside of taking charge of my own development.

New opportunities to learn and grow on the job are always available. We just need to look for them, recognize them, and then begin to grow in relation to the need. It starts with deciding to become deliberately developmental.

What Is a Deliberately Developmental Individual?

Deliberately developmental individuals (DDIs)* are on the high end of the intersection between Clarity of Purpose and the internal Developmental Drive to grow and develop at work. Let's take a deeper look at the ways these two concepts can meet.

If *Clarity of Purpose* is on the left axis and *Developmental Drive* is along the bottom (see Figure 1), that gives us four quadrants with different orientations on development at work:

1. Little clarity and a weak drive for growth, resulting in feeling *disengaged.*

2. Little clarity and a strong drive for growth, resulting in *dabbling.*

3. Strong clarity but a weak drive for growth, resulting in *dutifully doing.*

4. Strong clarity with a strong drive for growth, resulting in *deliberate development.*

Being *Disengaged* from your development happens when you don't know what to do or if you really want to do it. You're not sure (yet) what is worth putting your efforts into. You may be somewhat interested in a lot of things, but you lack focus. There isn't much drive toward learning because you lack desire, hope, or direction. Or you may feel there is nothing you can do about it. Most of us have experienced seasons in our work that are like that—feeling as if we're "going through the motions."

---

* I adapted this idea from what Robert Kegan and Lisa Laskow Lahey call a DDO (a deliberately developmental organization) in their book *Immunity to Change: How to Overcome It and Unlock the Potential in Yourself and Your Organization* (Cambridge, MA: Harvard Business Review Press, 2009).

DUTIFUL DOER HIGH Clarity of Purpose LOW Developmental Drive	**DELIBERATELY DEVELOPMENTAL** HIGH Clarity of Purpose HIGH Developmental Drive
DISENGAGED LOW Clarity of Purpose LOW Developmental Drive	**DABBLER** LOW Clarity of Purpose HIGH Developmental Drive

CLARITY OF PURPOSE — HIGH / LOW

DEVELOPMENTAL DRIVE — LOW / HIGH

Figure 1

Sometimes people become disengaged to cope with burnout, failure, or disappointment. Or they "catch" this mindset like the flu from those around them. People who are disengaged show up to work, perform adequately, collect the First Paycheck, and focus on fulfillment outside of work.

A *Dabbler*, or what I like to call a "growth grazer," loves trainings and workshops—can't get enough of them—and is always into the "life hacks" expressed by the latest book or podcast. Dabblers are all about getting better at whatever they are into this month. In fact, if you are a Dabbler, you may already spend serious time on your learning activities. However, most Dabblers cannot tell you how their learning connects to what they want in life or out of their career. Lacking connection to a goal, purpose, or focus, the learning doesn't take them in the direction they want to go—or really in much of *any* direction beyond a joy of learning. They are hungry to learn and try new things, but have little idea of what the goal of their learning is.

Dutiful Doers, on the other hand, are the "workhorses" of many organizations. They have a deep sense of *why* they do what they do, and a great deal of conviction and devotion to a purpose or role, but are less interested in learning new approaches and growing themselves along the way. They are dutifully "head-down," checking off the tasks that need completing. They may have extensive technical expertise or great abilities in a specific area, but they are focused only on using what they know, not on learning anything new.

Those with a deliberately developmental orientation discover that not only does this approach to work offer them opportunities to grow job skills, but it also offers them opportunities to grow capabilities that can lead them to better lives.

These hard workers are relentless at taking the next step, and generally have blinders on that block out everything around them except the work that is right in front of them. Individuals with a Doer orientation are motivated by the importance of the mission of their role, but they don't see the bigger picture. While the world around them changes, they don't. Until those in this category recognize the importance of growing in order to optimize their potential, they limit themselves to what can be accomplished with the methods, knowledge, and skills they already possess. They block themselves from innovation and reinvention because of their disregard for development.

Once you add Clarity of Purpose to an already strong Developmental Drive, you have a *Deliberately Developmental* approach. This orientation leads people to grow on purpose, on an ongoing basis, no matter where they are in their organization, with or without a program or sponsor. They focus their learning on building the skills needed to do the work that furthers the causes they care about. They see where change is needed, whether it means a shift in perspective, new products, or modifications in workplace procedures. These folks cherish opportunities to grow and learn—opportunities found in new and more-challenging assignments. They want to work with those who hold different viewpoints. They want to think together with other professionals, take courses, and set aside specific times for professional development. They will make time to practice new techniques and models while they get their work done.

Those with a deliberately developmental orientation discover that not only does this approach to work offer them opportunities to grow job skills, but it also offers them opportunities to grow capabilities that can lead them to better lives. By experimenting with better ways to communicate on the job, they build better communication skills to use with family and friends, in their volunteer work, and in their personal projects. For instance, they may learn more about finances, and by doing so, build their skills to become treasurer at their favorite nonprofit. With a learning mindset applied to everyday activities, they gain more confidence in their abilities and an increased capacity to navigate myriad challenges.

But what if you lose that Developmental Drive, yet maintain a strong Clarity of Purpose in some area? Perhaps the most important thing to recognize about the four quadrants is that nothing is static or permanent. It's more of a continuum that you move along at different stages of engagement, rather than a fixed classification of "how you are." Because people choose to grow and change, the same person could move to different quadrants of development at different times in her career, or even in different aspects of the same role, depending on her willingness, interests, and context.

This book supports all these development perspectives through deliberate reflection on what you find most fulfilling.

In the following chapters you will notice new choices available to you, based on your perspective on purpose and development. Just like a good coach, this book will encourage you to take specific steps toward your desired future. It all begins in the same place. And it all begins with the decision to take charge of your own growth.

WHY Do the Reflection Exercises?

» To notice the ways in which you are already deliberately developmental.

» To be able to readily identify what helps you "bootstrap" your own professional growth.

» To see the connection between professional development and other areas of your life.

» To begin the initial planning for how you will grow in your current role.

REFLECTION EXERCISES

1. When you think about your past professional development, what percentage was sponsored by organizations you worked for compared to your own self-directed development efforts?

2. Think about your last professional "growth spurt." What prompted you to build new skills or competencies?

3. To what extent are your professional skills transferable to other areas in your life?

4. Where would you place yourself on the matrix of "Clarity of Purpose" and "Developmental Drive"? (And don't forget that you may be in different places in the different roles you play in your job and life.)

5. What kind of self-directed growth is possible in your work setting?

6. In what areas do you feel attracted to grow new skills, improve, or learn something new?

THE SHIFT:

"Feeling trapped by others' expectations"

"Owning your path forward."

2

YOUR DEVELOPMENTAL EDGE

Learning happens in the moment of uncertainty.
The barrier that protects a person's sense of self
and the world is momentarily breached,
leaving the person vulnerable enough to learn.

—MARCIA REYNOLDS
author of *The Discomfort Zone*

WHEN DIANE WAS PROMOTED to team leader of her division at a growing solar energy company, she thought she was on her way up. She'd been there for twelve years, and her performance reviews had always been stellar. She was constantly recognized as a person with "high potential" in all of her reviews, except the most recent one. For the first time, Diane received criticism for her performance, and it felt personal.

She suddenly felt she was stagnating. It seemed like younger colleagues were advancing faster than she was—many of whom she had trained. They were getting raises; she wasn't. Diane felt cheated. She'd given her heart and soul to her job, and that no longer seemed appreciated. Her confusion, anger, and resentment were making her miserable.

Diane's manager asked her to seek coaching because he didn't know what else to do with her. He explained that she seemed moody and critical and unable to coordinate well with others. That's how she came to me. I learned she was highly knowledgeable, which was a great strength to draw on as we looked for other areas where she could grow. I asked her about her frustrations and the critiques from her recent review. Her manager had requested she do a better job communicating with her team, improve her work/life balance, and work on her mood. (She was often short-tempered and seemed joyless.) Her negative mood spread stress and irritation to others, and her manager had to deal with the fallout of those interactions.

Diane explained to me that she probably received this evaluation because she had been short with some junior employees. She'd found herself having to do work for them because they were not reliable. This only increased the pressure she was under. The last time she took a vacation, an entire project she was working on fell apart while she was away. It took weeks to right the ship once she returned. She felt she was single-handedly carrying the team's workload and was afraid to take any more time off. As a result, because the company had a "use it or lose it" vacation policy, Diane found herself losing time she had earned. She felt trapped and couldn't figure out what else to do—except stay focused on keeping projects going and getting stuff done.

"How do I fix this?" she asked me.

The A-W-S Cycle

Diane was at the start of a typical growth cycle. The process of growing in our roles, regardless of job level, has similar basic characteristics. Knowing this structure allows us to have greater control of the pace and type of development that takes place for us. It's like having a map.

Knowing what matters to us as individuals gives us greater clarity for how fast we are looking to grow—the route and speed of the trip—and which direction that growth should take us. The cycle goes like this:

Building Awareness

Awareness is the first key to growth. It's the point at which you discover something that is holding you back. In a lot of ways, this is the first step in being a "conscious" professional (as opposed to those who sleepwalk through their careers). Awareness lets you recognize what is at issue and opens up a world of different paths forward. Awareness can be painful, because it forces us to see how *we* are hampering *ourselves*.

New levels of awareness are often sparked by a problem or challenge like the one Diane faced. I know that many of us would like to feel "done" with our inner work, like it's all in the past, but that's not how we get better at what we do and have more influence. Becoming aware often triggers our defenses. It can expose our thinking as incomplete or faulty. It shows us weaknesses our strengths can't make up for. But it's worth confronting the ways we are not yet living into our best selves, not walking the talk, and/or not living our values. In turn, embracing new awareness gives us control because it reveals the potential to shift what we need to in order to achieve new outcomes.

Such shifts make all the difference. They help us see ourselves differently and bring new perspective of our role in relation to others. Allowing ourselves to be shaped by greater awareness shows us a way to move forward. One of the best tools for opening ourselves to awareness is reflection, which opens doors to the growth we need to fully serve the causes we care about.

Until Diane's review and the critical comments in it, she had no idea anything was wrong. She knew she'd been a bit short with her direct reports in a few instances, but other than that, no one was criticizing her work. In fact, many colleagues commiserated with her about the challenges of younger workers getting promoted. Those around her fed into the notion that she was being "wronged"—a victim of the company's policies and changes in the workplace. Few knew—and none had the courage to say—that she was playing a role in exacerbating the situation.

Through taking time to pause and consult with a coach (the same process could have been done through regular journaling and/or having a thinking partner), Diane was able to follow the frustration to its source: Some staff she had trained were getting promoted while she was not—and there might be a legitimate reason. Only then could she see that her attitude—and some of her Doer mentality—was getting in the way of her being a leader and an inspiration to her team. Her lack of patience and mentoring skills hampered her ability to instill the same standard for excellence in her team that she demanded of herself. She did too much of the work herself, which only fed her frustration, and others' frustration with her.

But was she up to the task of changing those behaviors?

Cultivating Willingness

Willingness puts our awareness into action. It takes the exciting or painful realizations awareness can bring and transforms them into a positive force. If others are to blame, what is ours to do? *Not much.* That mindset tends to make us feel helpless. But we can figure out a way to move forward, a way that puts us in charge. Restraining our initial knee-jerk reaction that someone else is to blame, we can create the space for choice, *if* we decide to try. When we are willing, we can choose to change ourselves first—forging a path to undiscovered country, with new responses and new approaches to shift the circumstances around us for the better.

But not all who are aware are willing. Nor should they be.

Some people become aware of things that need to change, and rather than addressing them, they become paralyzed. They don't want to do the work. They don't want to stretch in new ways, and they don't want to grow. Rather than confronting, they hide in the comfort of what they already know and how they have behaved in the past. Rather than fighting to change, they flee—emotionally, intellectually, or physically, or maybe all three. Or they stay and fight to remain unchanged. They continue to see the world through the lenses that they are familiar with—the ones that justify their actions—and they blame others. Fear and resistance can create a large gap between recognizing a shortcoming and doing something about it. Cultivating willingness closes that gap.

When Diane was presented with the cost of sticking to her old behaviors in her new position—such as lowering her chance of promotion by remaining comfortably in her area of mastery (see Figure 1), or having little time to do the big-picture work of a leader due to being trapped in a cycle of doing other people's work for them—she closed the willingness gap very quickly. It took courage to admit she didn't know how to work in any other way. But when she thought about not being able to take vacation again, she cultivated the will to move past her discomfort and build the skills necessary to run a team.

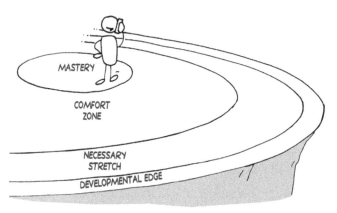

Figure 1

She began to see the skills she needed to develop, such as learning how to successfully delegate, knowing when to step back and train rather than step in to do, and how to calm herself in frustrating circumstances in order to respond professionally rather than emotionally. Now that she was willing, there was a lot to be gained. She began thinking about how to make room in her schedule to work on these areas.

What you are willing and not willing to do reveals your values. We don't all value moving into a leadership role. If you value technical innovation, for instance, you would be interested in what it takes to get good at that. We choose with our willingness to invest in some areas of growth and not in others. This direction, which comes from your self-awareness, can help you decide where to spend your time and effort—and where not to. The key is allowing your willingness to be shaped by what really matters—and not your fears, gripes, or lack of imagination.

Developing Skills

Developing new skills and capabilities is a strategic response to a challenge. It's one thing to solve a problem; it's another to change your behavior, perceptions, or the environment so that the same problem is never a challenge again.

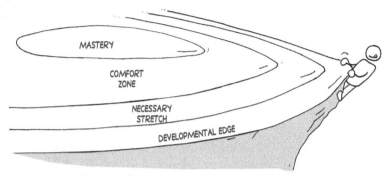

Figure 2

For Diane, learning to delegate and train was an uncomfortable process. She felt, at times, like she was dangling at her developmental edge by a fingerhold (see Figure 2). She realized that the only way she was going to grow was to temporarily step away from the center of her circle of mastery. Moving away from what she already knew how to do opened up new territory. She was going to have to try some things she hadn't before and would probably make some mistakes, but at least that would mean she was moving toward what she really wanted, rather than stagnating where she was. What seemed the edge of her abilities at first became just an uncomfortable stretch, and then something she could do without trouble, and, eventually, a more natural habit.

A couple months later, she felt she could go on vacation for the first time in years. When she came back from Spain and things were still intact, she was able to attack her role with renewed vigor instead of needing to patch things back together as she had before. The hope she'd had of focusing more of her attention at the system level was being realized. The changes she made gave her work—and her life—new meaning. Now, instead of avoiding areas that had been uncomfortable for her, she began to look for blind spots or problem points she could leverage into new growth. It really changed the game for her.

"There Are Only Possibilities"

One of the few quotes on my office wall reads:

We find what we look for

I use this quote to remind myself that there is almost always a positive outcome *if only I will look for it*. It increases my awareness of opportunities and the potential of situations and people to propel me toward my desired future, even if my initial reaction was frustration or anger that the outcome didn't meet my expectations.

We need to know what we are looking for.

What are you looking for?

What do you need to reach the future you want?

Are there elements of what you need that might be hidden within what you are facing right now? For instance, what skills are available for you to learn while you do your current job? Could you be learning project management, contracting, people management, facilitation skills, or industry history right where you are? Which of those skills are closest to something you'll need to do in your desired future?

If it's not obvious, perhaps looking at it from a new angle will reveal something you can work on to make a difference. Moving from the stimulus of *what we don't want* into thoughts about *what we do want* turns roadblocks into pathways. Setbacks become new footholds from which to push forward. This mindset uses awareness to reveal new realms, new possibilities, and new areas to cultivate willingness to grow.

Do the Reflection Exercises?

> » To identify your developmental edge in specific areas and notice what happens for you internally when you approach one.

> » In order to see self-directed development as a natural cycle that you can master.

> » To take charge of your own professional growth.

> » So you can learn from past successes.

REFLECTION EXERCISES

1. Have you been out on a developmental edge recently? What feelings do you notice when you get near a developmental edge?

2. Where at work or in your home life have you experimented with building new skills or getting better at something? What prompted you to start testing new approaches?

3. How are you currently gaining awareness about new areas where you'd like to grow?

4. Willingness helps us determine what matters to us and where it makes sense to invest. How do you decide what is worth working on?

5. When was the last time you felt stuck and then were able to work through it? How did you get unstuck? What strategies have worked well for you in making such grow changes?

6. What new abilities and/or skills are most important for you to develop right now?

THE SHIFT:

"Staying focused on
what I'm already good at"

"Pushing my boundaries
to discover
what I'm capable of."

THE NECESSARY STRETCH

I always did something I was a little not ready
to do. I think that's how you grow. When there's
that moment of "Wow, I'm not really sure I can
do this," and you push through those moments,
that's when you have a breakthrough.

—MARISSA MAYER
youngest woman ever listed in *Fortune* magazine's annual list
of America's Fifty Most Powerful Women in Business

I'VE ALWAYS LOOKED UP TO Frances Hesselbein.[2] She was
the CEO of the Girl Scouts of the USA when I first heard about her.
She's a marvel. Early in my career, I followed what she was doing
as much as I could. I read her books. I read books by other people
that described her leadership style. I subscribed to the journal she
edited. When I faced decisions, I imagined what she might do,
trying to channel her advice. I tried to absorb her guidance, even
though we had never met.

Then, one of my first clients asked for my help to find a speaker
on leadership development for public health executives. My first
thought was, "Who would be better than Frances?"

Of course, I didn't know Mrs. Hesselbein, nor did I have any contacts who did, but out of my desire to have a truly profound impact on these executives, and perhaps a bit of naïveté, I crafted a letter to her, noting the concepts in her recent magazine columns and inviting her to support these public healthcare leaders by talking with them about her leadership methods.

Amazingly, a little over a week later, I received a letter from her. She agreed to come speak for us.

It was one of those moments of extreme exhilaration and complete terror at the same time. *She agreed to come speak for us!* Then, *Holy moly, I'm going to meet Frances Hesselbein! What am I going to wear? What will I say? How is this going to work?* I had no idea, but I kept moving forward.

In the following weeks we finalized the details and determined that she would deliver a short speech, followed by a relaxed, living-room-style question and answer session that I would facilitate. We would be sitting in upholstered chairs like on a talk show, and I would interview her.

What came next was the brutal internal backlash that so often accompanies stretching toward the developmental edge. My thoughts started digging into my insecurities: *I'm going to interview Frances Hesselbein? In front of my first major client? What was I thinking? You have no experience interviewing people! You're going to embarrass yourself! And Frances will be sorry she agreed. I don't know how to make this turn out okay! Why did I get myself into this?* (I imagine you know the drill and have your own version of negative self-talk.)

Luckily, my bouts of panic rarely last long. In fact, the fear and doubt challenged me. I drove myself to do what I needed to do to make this valuable for everyone involved, or at least to do my best to increase the likelihood that it would turn out okay.

The first thing I could think of was to research anyone else who had interviewed her. I found a fellow who interviewed key-note speakers and had interviewed Frances the year before. With nothing to lose and very much to gain, I called him—expressing that I was going to interview Frances Hesselbein and my genuine desire, out of respect for her, to have the skills to ensure that her message would be well received by this group. I asked if he would take a few minutes to coach me. Blessedly, he agreed and took twenty minutes to tell me, a stranger, the basics of his craft. His guidance was excellent. It improved the experience for all involved. I am still grateful for his kindness.

Now that I understood how to conduct the session, my focus turned to looking the part. I asked a professional image consultant to help me figure out how to make my college-thrift-store (and barely functional) wardrobe work. (It didn't. I had to buy a new suit.) Increasing my professional poise and presence was a great way to not just look, but also feel, like I could do this successfully.

Frances Hesselbein frequently says, "Leadership is a matter of how to *be*, not how to *do*." I can't say I fully understood the meaning until I experienced her in person. She had no entourage. She was clearly a senior citizen, a tiny lady, and she wore cherry-red patent leather pumps and matching lipstick. Wow. But none of that mattered. It was all about the feeling I experienced in her presence. It was palpable.

I found her to be calm, supportive, and curious, and I didn't want to disappoint her. It was an honor to be near her and absorb her positive energy. When she spoke to me, it felt like love was emanating from her. I had never experienced anything like that. And, at the end of our very successful session for public health executives, I was in tears as I helped her into her taxi. I didn't want her to go; I wanted to climb into the cab with her. The client standing by my side also welled up and hugged me as Frances drove away. She felt it too.

None of that would have been possible had I not leapt out of my comfort zone, beyond my level of skill and knowledge, and followed up with the hard work of making myself as ready as I could.

Choosing to Have a Growth Mindset

In her TEDx talk titled "The Power of Yet,"[3] Dr. Carol Dweck speaks of a high school in Chicago where students are required to pass a certain number of courses to graduate. When they don't earn high enough marks, the students are not told they failed the course. Instead, they receive a grade of "Not yet." As Dr. Dweck put it, "If you get a failing grade, you think, 'I'm nothing; I'm nowhere.' But if you get the grade 'not yet,' you understand that you are on a learning curve. It gives you a path into the future."

Dr. Dweck has made a career out of seeing how people, especially children, cope with challenge and difficulty. For her, "Not yet" reflected something she has found to be true over and over again. When faced with something a little too difficult for them, people tend to have two responses:

1. "Awesome! An opportunity to try something new and learn!" or

2. "Oh my gosh, if I fail, people are going to know I'm not that smart. Let me figure a way out of this."*

Dr. Dweck labels those individuals who see challenges as "learning opportunities" as people who have a "growth mindset."

---

* If you are interested in learning some of the science and research that has led Dr. Dweck to these conclusions, I highly recommend her book *Mindset: The New Psychology of Success* (Ballantine Books, 2007).

They see themselves as malleable beings in the process of becoming something greater than they are now. Any problem is solvable given enough time to focus on it, and each opportunity to tackle such a challenge is an opportunity to grow. Failures are merely stepping stones to eventual success, based on refining and trying new methods. Success is a process of overcoming obstacles and is impossible to attain without confronting challenges.

In contrast to this, Dr. Dweck says the second group has what she calls a "fixed mindset." They see their intelligence and skillset as static and somewhat permanent. They are trapped in the "tyranny of now," which tells them, "What you know now is all there is and the best you can do. Manage it wisely." In other words, they don't see challenges as opportunities to grow—because they don't really believe they can change. What the first group sees as an opportunity, they see as risks that might expose that they really aren't that clever or capable.

Any problem is solvable given enough time to focus on it, and each opportunity to tackle such a challenge is an opportunity to grow.

As human beings, we like to be sure of things. We are attracted to that which makes us feel certain, even when it traps us in a place with limited potential. Fixed-mindset folks believe talent is something that is bestowed at birth and determines one's fate, while those with a growth mindset see innate talent, no matter how limited, as merely a starting point. It's what one *does* with what one *has* that really matters.

These are not just philosophical differences of opinion. This belief about whether we can grow, or not, is a fundamental driver of behavior that tends to prove self-fulfilling.

There are some interesting differences between groups of people who hold the "power of not yet" perspective versus those who hold the "tyranny of now" viewpoint. When Dr. Dweck asked students who had failed what they would do in facing similar challenges in the future, those with a fixed mindset didn't speak of improvement over time. Several with a fixed mindset said they would look for people who had done worse than they did so they could feel better about themselves. Others spoke of finding a way to opt out. Some said they might find a way to cheat. Those with a growth mindset talked of what they could do between now and then to be better prepared.

In study after study, Dr. Dweck has found those with fixed mindsets tend to run from difficulties. As they confronted challenges, they usually shut down rather than attack the problems with vigor. These people are more likely to go with what was successful in the past rather than try new things. They look for approval or consolation rather than push the envelope of their potential. They ignore constructive criticism, need constant validation, and therefore see the success of others as diminishing their own.

If we combine the mental filter of our career aspirations with a growth mindset, however, we can see opportunities and new pathways forward, rather than stumbling blocks. It's the difference between saying, "I can't do that" and "I can't do that yet—but I'll figure it out." It's literally the difference between quitting and persisting.

So how do we harness the power of "not yet"?

When you push yourself out of your comfort zone to learn something new and difficult, the neurons in your brains fire to form new, stronger connections around that new pattern. This process of changing how our neurons fire makes us better at new things every time that pattern is repeated. Dr. Dweck describes how the knowledge of these brain functions transforms how students think about challenges. She says, "Before, effort and difficulty made them feel dumb—made them feel like giving up. But now, effort and difficulty—that's when their neurons are making new connections, stronger connections—that's when they're getting smarter."[4]

Growing While You Work

Because our workplaces often provide our greatest challenges, they can become places to grow as a human being. The fulfillment of a job well done comes best when we've increased our skills in the process of succeeding at a difficult task by transforming the meaning of the work challenges we faced. Each time we do that, we upgrade how we see ourselves as well. We make another micro-identity shift that increases our capacity—and desire—for growth.

Growing a business and working in a start-up have a lot in common with students dealing with challenging math problems. On one hand, I could view my failure to launch a product, or build a management team, or break five-million dollars in revenue as not having what it takes—that I am incapable of doing it. I could also look at it another way. By invoking the power of "not yet," I can see that my attempts thus far have given me more information, strengthened my sense of what is needed, and driven me to grow in a new way, because I haven't figured it out *yet*. But I will, if I keep at it.

Dealing with a range of "growth" or "stretch" issues over time has built my confidence. Even when the next steps aren't exactly clear, I like the picture of the future better on the other side of learning from the experience. Additionally, I like variety. Once I get through this part, I can move on to have other experiences and conduct other experiments. People who place a high value on being able to learn new things are not well served by a fixed mindset, because it limits how they perceive their options.

People who place a high value on being able to learn new things are not well served by a fixed mindset, because it limits how they perceive their options.

A wise friend of mine calls this drive to keep going "relentless forward progress." He talks about it in the context of long-distance running. Ultra-marathoners use this to stay laser focused on taking the next, and the next, and the next step forward. For me, it has become a mantra that encapsulates the power of "yet" and the growth mindset that seeks to keep moving forward, using everything at our disposal to improve ourselves. In the process, we grow our identity as we discover new layers of what we can do and who we can become.

Do the Reflection Exercises?

» In order to see how a growth mindset applies to your work.

» To leverage what works for you when it's time to stretch out of a comfort zone.

» To identify and arrange for support as you grow new skills.

» So you can make the micro-identity shift to seeing yourself as a learner.

REFLECTION EXERCISES

1. Recall a time when you stretched into new areas beyond your comfort zone.
   a. What prompted the stretch?
   b. How did you learn or grow yourself to be able to do what was needed?
   c. How did it turn out?
   d. Today, what do you conclude about that stretch experience?

2. Can you think of people in your work or home life who demonstrate a "fixed mindset"? What impact does their approach have on you?

3. Can you think of people in your work or home life who demonstrate a "growth mindset"? What impact does their approach have on you?

4. How can you employ the "power of not yet" in areas that are hard for you?

5. How do you ask for support or help from others when you don't know quite how to tackle a new challenge? Explore some examples by describing them and how they turned out.

6. What would help support you while you are stretching to learn and do more?

THE SHIFT:

—FROM—

"Who I am now is
who I'll always be"

—TOWARD—

"Who I am evolves
as I am able to do more."

TRANSFORMATION AT WORK

There is always a step small enough from
where we are to get us to where we want to be.
If we take that small step, there's always another
we can take, and eventually a goal thought to be
too far to reach becomes achievable.

—DR. ELLEN LANGER
the first female psychology professor
to be granted tenure at Harvard

I WAS IN THE MIDST of writing this chapter when I got a call from Jean. It had been four years since we'd worked together. I'd served as her leadership coach for several years, facilitating team retreats and providing consulting to her organization. We parted ways because she'd taken a position with a hospital that did only internal leadership coaching. She was calling because she'd transitioned to a new role with a national nonprofit and was wondering about the opportunity to work together again. It was good to catch up.

As we chatted, I asked her how things were going at the hospital. It sounded like things had gone well, but Jean is modest.

As I pressed a little more, she shared the following about her time there:

One of the first things I did was investigate what resources for coaching and team assessment we had available to us. While I was disappointed to learn you were not on the approved list of coaches, I was pleased to see some of the tools you coached me on were.

I did the DISC behavior assessment[5] with our team. This tool provides a profile about how people behave in different ways— some are more dominant, others more analytical, and so on. It respects and values the differences among people that make a team strong.

By bringing that concept in early and doing it in such a way that didn't overwhelm, it allowed us to have honest and meaningful conversations as a team, and we could understand each other. We were able to move along quickly through the conversations we needed to have.

Because we took care of the interpersonal, I was able to focus our attention on the ultimate impact of the work—serving the patients that are enrolled in our healthcare system. We were able to address things like "What would be a true indicator that we were really making an impact on the welfare of our patients?" "How could we measure that?" "Were we able to reduce cancer?" Or "Did we improve cancer-screening rates?" "Did we somehow contribute to clinicians' adopting a new technology or some other valuable tool in quality of care?"

I was able to help the team get past their tendency to sit around the table and fight with one another about things like "I can't get my workforce project done because such and such won't . . ." or "My project is roadblocked because you x-y-z-ed." We got *way* past issues like "So-and-so didn't say hello to me this morning, so now I'm going to be nasty all day."

Whenever we had problems, or we lost our way, I would hear your voice saying things like "But look, all these are opportunities. Let's prioritize them." Or "Okay, let's look at the bigger picture behind that and connect the dots back to this issue."

We moved from individuals working in silos to team members who saw their collective impact. That was because we did very deliberate strategic planning, and we thought together continuously.

As a result, we built a reputation for being able to pivot and respond creatively to different situations. We were seen as credible, innovative, willing to partner, flexible, and ultimately able to get to the best outcomes for our patients quickly.

Before I left, they gave me a lovely going-away celebration. In front of the whole group, one of the team members said, "Jean, we would sometimes get frustrated with how many times you would ask 'why?' It was worth it, because ultimately, the products that come out of this office now and the work that we're doing is of the highest quality and has made us all better healthcare professionals." That was pretty affirming.

And it's not like the level of quality has gone down since I left either. Last Wednesday morning I had coffee with my deputy, who took over for me when I left, and he said, "You'd be proud, Chief. Everything's rolling along; we're doing well."

I smiled to myself, flashing back to one of my first meetings with her. Jean sure was different back then. She had just been promoted to her first management role. We worked on her interactions with peers and direct reports, on increasing her influence and skill at orchestrating the efforts of a diverse team in achieving big goals, and on her communications outwardly and up to ensure her team received recognition for their work. She dealt with some cantankerous senior managers, and then succession planning as they transitioned out. She believed in herself enough to risk leading through these situations, learning from her missteps, and gradually built her confidence as a result.

By the time Jean was ready to take on the next role, and then the next one, she had built a pattern of growing herself and her team to deliver consistently positive results. One microshift at a time, she changed the leader she saw herself as, and what she was capable of delivering for her organization, her team, and herself.

Unfortunately, though, most don't embrace the challenge to grow on the job like Jean did, and still does. Why is that?

Why Do We Resist Change?

Harvard professors Robert Kegan and Lisa Laskow Lahey leverage recent brain research and adult development to explain that as we get older, we can create entirely new levels of understanding and perspective, levels that aren't even possible for those who are younger. While most psychologists focus on development *into* adulthood, Kegan and Lahey explore the three stages of adult development that happen beyond our university years. Whether you are younger or older, this is good news! We are not "done" with our education or formation as human beings when we get out of school and go to work. We're not "fixed" (as we've already discussed), but can continue to grow to address the incredibly complex problems our societies face. Young-adult dichotomies of black and white transform into rainbows of different approaches for understanding and interacting with the world around us as we mature. This continued development is necessary if we are going to open the door to creating new and better solutions.

Yet, even when it is literally a matter of life or death, the ability to change remains challenging, mysterious, and sometimes out of reach. People stay attached to their current identity, habits, and approaches even when they have documented negative consequences. For instance, a recent medical study showed that when heart doctors tell seriously at-risk patients they will die if they don't change their personal habits, only one in seven follow through to successful change.[6]

Why? When choosing A means living longer and choosing B means more health complications, why do these people stick with the B choices that got them into their predicament in the first place? Because, underneath it all and beyond their conscious desires, they cling to the *nothing is wrong* identity. Not wanting to see themselves as sick, they refuse to change their habits. Regardless of the risk, identity holds sway. Change can't happen until *they are willing to see themselves differently.*

If we want to reach our potential and gain new insights from our experiences, we must upgrade our identity.

How we see ourselves *matters*. If we want to reach our potential and gain new insights from our experiences, we must upgrade our identity. Each incremental identity upgrade is a micro-identity shift that allows us to shape who we become. If you feel you have no choice in your identity and it's just "who you are," this is a great place to begin to see more options to transform yourself. Behaviors or habits we want to change are not "bad" or "wrong." They are choices we have made in the past, and we can become a person who chooses differently going into the future.

Potential—especially leadership potential—is realized as we understand that our choices matter. Decisions define leadership. Each micro-identity shift builds new potential for us.

The Power of Deliberately Developmental Shifts

For those who wish to deliberately develop themselves to meet the demands of their personal mission, micro-identity shifts create an evolving sense of self in which we have slightly new intentions, slightly new levels of understanding, and a resolve to experiment with slightly new approaches every day. Whether we've had work experiences that strengthened our self-confidence or traumatic events we've had to recover from, we build meaning and become more fully ourselves based on how we interpret what happened. Sometimes we grow because we set our sights on a positive future, and sometimes we make shifts because we never want to experience the same ordeals again. How we choose to see our current and past challenges drives the impact they have on our evolving capabilities and identity.

Why be limited by what you were able to dream yesterday?

New experiences build new proficiencies and possibilities. In relation to these external changes, we may experience small shifts in how we see ourselves internally—tiny modifications in our identity. Previously we weren't able to do X. Now we are able to do X, and we're getting better at Y. This causes us to update our sense of who we are as human beings and takes us a tiny step closer to who we want to become.

By self-directing your learning, you become capable of so much more each year. It would be a shame to lock yourself into a previous version of your potential. Why be limited by what you were able to dream yesterday? Deliberately developmental professionals keep getting better because they are committed to their own growth, are interested in overcoming new challenges, and enjoy building their capacity to do more. They are curious to find better ways to do whatever it is they do and to reimagine the possibilities of their potential.

If you think back over your career—however long or short—you will notice times when your sense of what you are capable of shifted. You may not have seen yourself as a leader at first, but you found yourself acting as one. Eventually an updated identity—as a competent leader able to make decisions, speak up, and address complex problems—catches up with your skills, one small, incremental shift at a time.

Growing a business has required me to grow up again and again. Each time my team bumps into a limitation of how we have set up our structures, partnerships, and planning, I find it's time for me to grow myself up just a bit more. Then that growth is reflected in the results we are able to achieve together as a team. Someone on staff once joked, "I just saw you evolve like a Pokémon—right there you transformed!"

Since our workplaces have a constant stream of challenges and changes, we can use them to bootstrap our internal development. They give us a never-ending stream of opportunities to grow. Sara Blakely, the founder and owner of Spanx (and one of the youngest self-made billionaires), put it this way: "Embrace what you don't know, especially in the beginning, because what you don't know can become your greatest asset." Sara turned her frustration about a product that she wanted, but didn't exist, into an enterprise, one persevering step at a time.

Growth comes by pausing and reflecting on why we do what we do, and what we have just been through. When we take a knee-jerk, autopilot response and bring it under review, it gives us new perspective. Looking at situations more objectively, we can choose what we want to do with them: Is our response a reflex we want in our lives or not? Is it consistent with our values? Do we want to change how we perceive and respond to this stimulus in the future? Is there something we need to learn or practice to be able to better address it?

We grow each time we do this and incrementally change who we are in the process. What is authentic and genuine evolves us toward the person we want to be, toward a more genuine and capable self. Each time we do this, it's perfectly legitimate to "update the file" we keep on ourselves and our capabilities and allow our self-identities to grow toward self-actualization.

Many small shifts added up are how we change positions or careers, break into new markets, or build the courage to try what we could not have done before. This inner transformation of a gradually shifting and evolving identity is reinforced by the outer transformation of our abilities. This is how we transform our work experience and the impact we can have on the world around us.

WHY Do the Reflection Exercises?

» To notice where change creates an identity shift in you.

» So you can appreciate the positive observations others have made about you.

» To recognize the costs and benefits of not making change.

» In order to explore how seeing yourself differently changes what you see around you.

REFLECTION EXERCISES

1. When you think about who you were ten years ago, compared to now, what has changed? What has stayed the same? How have you grown yourself as a professional?

2. What shifts in identity have occurred?
   Try completing these sentences:
   a. In the past I was . . .
   b. My identity shifted when . . .
   c. I'm currently in the process of shifting . . .

3. If there are some habits you are having a hard time changing, notice that you probably had a good reason for choosing these habits in the past. Do the benefits of keeping those habits outweigh the cost of changing them?

4. As you experience micro-identity shifts, how might that impact your perceptions of the events and people that come your way?

5. Many people have a hard time seeing themselves objectively. What positive observations do others share about you that you have a hard time accepting?

6. How might you celebrate one of your micro-identity shifts, one that enables you to make a greater difference for the causes you care about?

THE SHIFT:

—FROM—

From "I don't have time
to reflect at work"

—TOWARD—

"Reflection creates insights
that make work better."

5

THE POWER OF REFLECTION

If you follow your heart, if you listen to your gut,
and if you extend your hand to help another,
not for any agenda, but for the sake of humanity,
you are going to find the truth.

—ERIN BROCKOVICH
environmental activist

A FREQUENT BUSINESS FLIER, Jane found she thought best
during "plane time." She could look out over the cloudscape and
literally get a 30,000-foot view as a backdrop for her big-picture
thinking. After discovering this, she looked for ways to incorporate
similar elements in a more regular practice. Now she visits the top
floor of a nearby library with a fantastic view of a river stretching
toward the horizon, where she can sit down with pen and paper.
She takes this time to consider, write, ask, listen within, and think
through whatever is on her mind. Whether in an actual plane or
"flying" from the top floor of the library, Jane carves three blocks
of time a week out of her schedule to sit and consider her work and
the challenges she is facing.

In contrast, Don likes to walk. He poses a question to himself or decides on a problem he wants to address before he sets out, and then contemplates those items as he strolls along a familiar path. He considers metaphors from nature as he reviews different perspectives on an issue. He repeatedly reminds himself to breathe deeply and enjoy the bird calls, sunshine, and sights around him to keep himself relaxed. When he returns to the office, he takes ten to fifteen minutes to capture his insights in his journal.

Rachel loves to go to her favorite coffee shop. She orders a chai and heads to a comfy chair with an end table. She puts on her headphones, listens to instrumental music, sips her chai, and waits. When she's in the groove, it seems like the thoughts just pour out. The thoughts lead to questions, and she begins to write out her reflections in response, one by one. She finds this is the best way to give herself a clear, dispassionate analysis of each alternative response to the events of her week. She thinks about the soundtrack as her virtual "thinking cap" when she listens and focuses. It helps her tap into productive ideas for how to address whatever's on her mind.

Karen does it completely differently. She likes to sit on a cushion to meditate for twenty minutes each morning and evening. She started doing this as a stress-reduction technique but found that it made her thinking clearer. She felt calmer and more in control of herself and her life when she stayed faithful to her practice. Taking regular time to be still, think her own thoughts, and clear her mind allowed her to relax into "being" instead of "doing." This time was an investment in her peace of mind and helped her stay on track with her goals. If something was out of whack in her work or home experience, it usually popped up during these times, and she would just sit with the issue and emotions, letting them flow as nonjudgmentally as she could. Some thoughts surprised her, but she didn't censor the "crazy" ideas. She just let them take shape and morph into another version. Some of her most innovative ideas were generated from this open-minded reflection. At the end of each session, she answers a set of questions in her journal.

Each of these reflection examples shows the power of finding your own unique way to enhance the value of your thinking. One of Albert Einstein's gifts was to think so clearly and precisely that it allowed him to make discoveries in his mind. He called these "thought experiments." Einstein's insights from thinking led to his theory of relativity. Taking time to think deeply and carefully—which can be called "reflection," "mindful inquiry," or as the Dalai Lama calls it, "analytical meditation"—can change our understanding in ways that are truly profound. With each new understanding, we have different options and actions from which to choose. In this way, our deep reflection in the present can shape our future.

Creating a Rhythm of Reflection

Reflection holds up a mirror and lets us see ourselves, who we really are, and what really matters to us. We hear our inner struggles, and if we can maintain perspective, we can see the thought patterns for what they are: choices about where to focus, different interpretations of an event, and ideas for what to do next—some of which are truly useful, and some of which are not. Looking in on our thinking gives us a chance to pause the action and explore more options.

Insights may also occur to us in a flash when we are doing something else. An idea bubbles up or pops into our mind. This is not the same as a practice of reflection, but it is likely an outcome of it. Many scientists use the power of the unconscious mind to contemplate problems they are trying to solve. They often start with a deliberate reflection or thought experiment to activate the deeper levels of their minds. Then they focus elsewhere. Out of the blue, a new idea emerges, creating an "aha" or "eureka" moment! It all started because they gave themselves time to reflect.

When we reflect, we can play out thought experiments for bolder approaches, courageous shifts, and do so *with no risk.* We can consider possibilities and allow our mental models to be stretched and expanded beyond our current comfort zone. The transformative power of imagination is well-documented, but we don't have to wait for someone to ask us good questions; we can ask ourselves during reflection time. When you use reflections and questions that help to reveal blind spots and gaps in logic, people instantly reframe situations and change. The pause in the action, with an objective focus, makes space to listen within for different potential responses and new ideas. It might raise issues we can add to our learning agendas—skills or practices for future research that will help us address those scenarios more competently.

Like the lumberjack who says, "I am too busy cutting down trees to take time to sharpen my saw," we risk putting forth unnecessary, unskillful effort if we don't make time to thoughtfully reflect on how to make changes for the better.

Opportunities for growth surround us every day, but too few take the time to notice them. It's a sad irony that we are often too busy doing to get better at doing. Like the lumberjack who says, "I am too busy cutting down trees to take time to sharpen my saw," we risk putting forth unnecessary, unskillful effort if we don't make time to thoughtfully reflect on how to make changes for the better.

Reflection takes time and saves time. It increases the efficiency of learning and enables strategic growth. Reflecting on your work experiences can help you gain more meaning, fulfillment, advancement, and positive impact. As David Boud, Rosemary Keogh, and David Walker write in their essay "Promoting Reflection in Learning: a Model": "The outcomes of reflection may include a new way of doing something, the clarification of an issue, the development of a skill, or the resolution of a problem."[7]

For this reason, I encourage people to take regular time away from *doing* to *reflect* and see if they can kick-start the awareness-willingness-skill cycle of growth for themselves. Reflection is the tool that pries us away from our constant running, doing, and screen viewing so we can engage in self-directed growth.

Many feel like they don't have the time for reflection. It's a common belief, but consider this: A research study spearheaded by Harvard Business School professors Francesca Gino and Gary Pisano found that individuals who stop to reflect on their process regularly are roughly 20 percent more efficient in the work they do than those who don't. The researchers conducted a set of experiments where participants were given a series of brainteasers and puzzles to solve in two sessions. A control group was given a first round of problems to solve, a break, and then a second round. Another group was asked to write down detailed reflections on the strategies they used between the two rounds. A third was given the same instructions as the reflection group, but was also informed that their notes would be shared with future participants.

The result was that the second two groups—the "reflection" and "sharing" groups—did almost 20 percent better than the group that just went back to work on the problems without any reflection time in between. And there was no significant difference between the "reflection" and "sharing" groups in their improvement. This research shows that reflection has tangible value to improve performance.[8] A 20 percent improvement would be like adding five more hours in your week. What could you accomplish with an extra twenty hours a month?

Just reflecting at the end of the day on what you learned can make a difference. In another experiment to evaluate the power of reflection, one group of study participants spent the last fifteen minutes of each day reflecting on what they had learned that day. A separate group of participants reflected, and then took an additional five minutes to explain their notes to another trainee. The control group simply continued to work. Over the course of a month, the reflection group preformed 22.8 percent better than the control group, while the sharing group performed 25 percent better, both despite having worked fifteen to twenty minutes less each day. The researchers concluded, "When we fall behind even though we're working hard, our response is often just to work harder. But in terms of working smarter, our research suggests that we should take time for reflection."[9]

It seems pretty obvious that not only is reflection time valuable, but if we are going to grow at work, it is essential. Margaret Wheatley, an accomplished writer on organizational behavior, weighs in on the consequences of not reflecting: "Without reflection, we go blindly on our way, creating more unintended consequences, and failing to achieve anything useful."

So how do we make reflection a habit?

By building reflection into the rhythm of our week.

It Won't Happen if You Don't Schedule It

Because reflection is so important, it is usually the first habit I recommend to clients to boost their Third Paycheck and become deliberately developmental at work. I suggest carving out at least three half-hour blocks during their week, and to find a quiet place to get away from everything else where they can do it. This is an appointment with their thoughts and reflections on what they are experiencing at work and any problems they are running into with people, systems, changes, or communication, as well as time to imagine new possibilities, ideas for improvement, opportunities, etc. I ask them to record everything in a journal.

The amount or frequency of reflection time is never a hard-and-fast rule, so any block of time one can find to devote to reflection is useful. Maybe at first, only once a week works until you experience the return on the time invested. For others, every day works better to maintain consistency. The point is to make a regular habit of the practice.

> *"Without reflection, we go blindly on our way, creating more unintended consequences, and failing to achieve anything useful."*
>
> —MARGARET WHEATLEY

A reflection practice can take myriad forms, but there is one thing that most methods have in common: At some point we want to pause and record our thoughts so we have them for future reference. Writing also has a way of helping us remember things.[10] In the same way that taking notes in class helps us learn—even if we never look at them again—recording our reflections is a powerful analytical aid. Once I have something down on paper, I find it makes room in my mind for the next layer of thoughts.

Like peeling an onion, journaling is one of the best practices for helping us mine the power of our own minds. A journal is the perfect place to refine your aspirations and aims. Having a written vision keeps you on track and allows you to review and add to your ideas. The evidence for clarifying and documenting your goals is overwhelmingly consistent. Just do it.

Your journal can be anything from a document you create on your computer, or an app, or a fine-embossed leather diary. It can be a three-ring binder, a spiral-bound notebook, or individual sheets of paper stapled together. Whatever suits you best is the best tool to use.

The key, of course, isn't what you use, but rather it's making reflection a habit.

WHY Do the Reflection Exercises?

> » To take an inventory of your current reflection practices.

> » So that you make the time for conscious reflection in your life.

> » In order to align with your inner guidance as you go about your work.

> » To figure out what type of reflection best suits your situation.

REFLECTION EXERCISES

1. When was the last time you set aside time to quietly notice your thoughts? How about what you are grateful for? Or what's going well for you right now?

2. Can you think of a time when pausing to reflect changed or improved a situation?

3. Are there pockets in your week where you could schedule a regular time to think and reflect?

4. What conditions would help support you to be consistent with the practice? How can you make sure your time isn't interrupted? Is there a favorite place for you to go?

5. What methods of thinking or listening work best for you when you need to gain perspective or temper your initial reaction?

6. How will you use the reflection questions in the upcoming chapters to spark your development?

We don't

see things

as they are,

we see them

as we are.

—ANAÏS NIN
author and essayist

PART TWO

THE AWARENESS SHIFTS

ATTAINING *awareness* is the starting point of your development cycle. Awareness increases your perceptual range, eliminates blind spots, and further awakens you to yourself, your circumstances, and the people and possibilities around you.

Increasing awareness is a never-ending quest of reflecting, learning, and distinguishing deeper layers of understanding and insight into the world around us.

THE SHIFT:

"It's frustrating
(or embarrassing) that I can't
make this work"

"If something bothers me,
it's because it matters—
and that's where I need to
up my game."

6

PAIN POINTS THE WAY

Somehow I always knew that
life gives endless new beginnings,
endless chances to remember
who you really are.

—TOSHA SILVER
Change Me Prayers

CORRINE HAD JUST been appointed to a big-deal committee that would make recommendations for upcoming state government decisions. Not only were the committee members well-known heads of organizations and subject-matter experts, the meetings were transcribed for public record. After the first meeting, Corrine read the transcript and was shocked at how disjointed her speaking came across. As a leader, she prided herself on being informal, friendly, and a connector who could untangle complex concepts. When she read the transcript, however, because of her word choice and sentence structure, her flow of ideas did not come through. She was embarrassed about being out of step with the other committee members. She had noticed that they spoke formally, but she didn't understand why until she read their remarks on paper.

Corrine sat down to think and wrote out some questions:

» What do I really want out of this situation?

» Why is it important?

» How can I turn my discomfort into productive action?

» What other options do I have?

» What can I realistically do between now and the next committee meeting?

» What help or support am I seeking?

After generating her list, she got up to fix a cup of her favorite tea, and then came back to review her thoughts. She checked in with herself to see if there was anything missing. Her gut told her, *Just get started.*

For the next thirty minutes, she wrote out responses.

Over the years, Corrine developed her own method for reflecting and finding answers to issues that confronted her. She would give herself a half hour to journal about her questions and see what actions and insights came from it. She usually finished feeling more confident and focused.

She also knew herself well enough to know that she was most successful in gaining mastery in a new area if she read about it, saw examples of people doing it, and then practiced it herself. She knew she'd be bad at it at first, but she was determined to use the practice as a learning experiment. She'd read articles about the neuroscience of learning—which confirmed that when you learn by doing, it activates the brain in a way that facilitates retention and mastery. She liked to do a little research first to get a leg up, which she split into "book knowledge" and "real-world examples."

After reflecting on her responses, she felt clearer about what she needed to do next. She wanted to gain more mastery as an impromptu speaker. She wanted to be on a committee like this in the future, and it seemed the perfect time to get better at being articulate on the fly. If she ever wanted to run for a public office, this would be a necessary skillset. Bringing her work opportunity to connect with her personal values, she could see how this situation was calling for her to lean into learning right where it hurt—in her lack of prowess at speaking on a committee when the proceedings were formal and transcribed.

She decided to monitor her progress by comparing the transcripts from one month to the next. Some meetings were recorded, so she watched a few and paid close attention to the speakers who were best on their feet. How did they enter into discussions? How did they organize their words? How did they give themselves time to think? What made their comments impactful? What lessened her effectiveness?

She read a couple of books about using her voice as a leader and recorded a couple of phone calls where she practiced what she was learning. Then she had those calls transcribed so she could read what she sounded like in print. She chuckled, thinking of her high school tennis coach saying, "Practice the way you want to play." That felt exactly like what she was doing.

At the next committee meeting, Corrine looked around the room, breathed deliberately a few times, and put what she'd been practicing into action. People listened. She felt they had heard and received what she shared. Thoughtful, knowledgeable people communicate effectively because they grow through their challenges.

"No One Listens to Me!"

Malcolm worked in an agency and was frustrated with the bureaucracy of getting *anything* done. "The management team is a tightly knit clique," he told me. "I can't get any traction. It just doesn't matter what I say. It doesn't matter what I put forward. They disregard it. I can't get any of my team's initiatives implemented!"

Malcolm had built his reputation on getting things done. It had gotten him this job. But for a person used to being in command, this new environment was a big shock. He felt disrespected. Worse yet, he felt he was letting his team down. "I can't do what my people need me to do to make this right," he confided. "What am I even doing here if I can't effect change?"

Malcolm's pain was letting him know that this was no place for business as usual.

One of the things I knew about Malcolm through our working relationship was that outside of work he dedicated a good deal of time to practicing jujitsu. Knowing a little about the martial art, I asked him, "If you were to approach this philosophically—like a problem with an opponent in jujitsu—what would you do first?"

He thought about that for a moment. "I'd look at my technique and try to eliminate the wasted energy. I might try a different move from a different angle. I'd look closely at what my opponent was doing and try to see why it was putting me off balance."

I let that sink in for a moment. "So where is your frustration coming from?"

I'd like to say he had an instant revelation and we solved the problem then and there, but development happens in small spurts of insights and takes time. We talked a good deal over the next hour about different approaches he might take.

Can we learn to love the pain that points the way? Or at least tolerate it, without trying to numb our feelings or blame someone else? Only by feeling the "ouch" can we translate it into something useful. Without allowing ourselves to explore the source of the pain, we may not focus on the salient issue.

In Malcolm's case, it turned out to be a question of his communication style. He was used to being the dominant figure in most conversations, especially in formal settings. When he acknowledged this, I asked him, "Which is more important to you: getting some traction for your team's initiatives or hanging on to that communication style?"

Without allowing ourselves to explore the source of the pain, we may not focus on the salient issue.

"Getting my team's initiatives some traction, of course."

"Well, then, what if you had someone else on your team present the ideas? What if, for example, you let one of the newer members step up and speak for your team?"

He didn't respond immediately, but I could tell it was something that had never occurred to him. I knew his hierarchical thinking was, *It's my idea. I am the boss. I have to present it.*

Rather than let the silence linger and let those thoughts derail him, I asked, "What if, as the leader of your division, it wasn't your job to be the tip of the spear, but to develop your team members to be able to handle that pressure as well as you do? What if you trained them to make the presentations and represent your team's ideas rather than always doing it yourself?"

That was a big shift for him, but also one he chose to embrace almost immediately. Building up other leaders to carry forth the message—what a great strategy to circumvent the barrier! Navigating through what at first appeared to be an impasse provided an entirely new prospectus for Malcolm to advance his leadership.

A few weeks later, when he asked one of his team members to present an initiative to a steering committee, he was pleased with both the reception it got and the perspective of being a bystander and watching one of his subordinates shine. It gave him a new reason to get out of bed every morning.

You Can't Learn from What You Don't Pay Attention To

In creating a career, taking on a new role, or rising to a new level in our companies, we don't know where our growing ground will be, but frequently pain will point the way to it. When you go to a doctor for an injury or ailment, one of her first questions is always, "Where does it hurt?" Once the general area is identified, the doctor is prone to poke and prod, asking over and over again, "Does this hurt? How about this? How about when I do this?" She's using pain to point the way to the problem.

"Wholeness does not mean perfection: it means embracing brokenness as an integral part of life."

—PARKER PALMER

We can use the same technique at work to figure out where we need to get better at what we do. A lot of people "play through the pain," thinking it's just part of the landscape of having a job, but when you start to pay attention, you'll become aware of the places you can not only grow professionally, but also make work more enjoyable and fulfilling. We don't realize an area requires attention until it starts to hurt. Then we see how we are limited by our lack of skill, knowledge, or mastery in that area. In those cases, pain points to where you can focus your learning to gain new capabilities.

As Parker Palmer wrote in *A Hidden Wholeness: The Journey Toward an Undivided Life*, "Wholeness does not mean perfection: it means embracing brokenness as an integral part of life." Sometimes we can power through our weaknesses by relying on our strengths. Other times, however, we need to confront our weaknesses and grow new skills so our nonstrengths don't trip us up on our career journeys.

For instance, you may identify with Corrine's story, as she experienced the pain of not being as good as she thought when speaking in public. Or you may identify with Malcolm's frustration at finding his usual approach to success was not helping him excel in his current workplace. Both of them used their pain to point the way to their next growing ground.

"Where Does It Hurt?"

There are two dimensions to letting our pain point the way. One is that we feel a stimulus that's not pleasant. The other is to ask ourselves why the discomfort matters to us. We tend not to experience pain over things we don't care about. Pain often points to something we value that is being compromised or dishonored. Malcolm cared about getting ideas moving forward to make change. Corrine cared about helping people understand complex concepts and holding her own with other experts in her field. They both experienced the pain of adversity *because they cared*. If they didn't care, they wouldn't be thinking about it, much less agonizing over it.

When pain comes from not getting the results we want in an area we care about, it's a call to action to map out our growing ground. Recognizing the pain provides an opportunity to create a learning agenda for getting better. What skills will allow you to address, alleviate, minimize, or somehow shift this pain from a problem to a new level of accomplishment? Unfortunately, at least initially, developing and learning won't alleviate the pain. However, they will allow us to grow into people who can look at the situation more objectively and tolerate it until we can eventually remedy the situation with a new approach or skillset. We have to allow pain to pave the path to insight.

When you venture out to the developmental edge for the sake of growing your ability to do what matters to you, you increase your field of mastery and are better able to trust yourself because of your new competencies. You can then draw on the new skills built for the rest of your life, both personally and professionally. This arc of growth stretches us into new territory, building new capability and developing our sense of accomplishment in new ways.

By paying attention to the pain we feel and using it productively, we expand our playing field. We can do more, change more, and have greater influence on the causes we care about. Directing our development to pinpoint the embarrassments, gaps in our abilities, and challenges that flare up for us is key to making a difference and taking home the Third Paycheck.

Do the Reflection Exercises?

» To identify ways to improve your work experience.

» To recognize that painful parts of your work might be a call to grow.

» So you can direct your development to make a real difference for you.

» To measure your developmental progress.

REFLECTION EXERCISES

1. List some areas where your work life hurts the most acutely.

2. Where does the pain originate? Why does it affect you? What matters to you about it?

3. Are there values you hold dear that are being compromised or dishonored in these situations?

4. Ideally, how would you like to see these situations improve?

5. What growth or development in your skills or approach would strengthen your ability to move these situations closer to the ideal?

6. How would you know if your skills were improving? What progress will you be looking for?

THE SHIFT:

—FROM—

"I must advocate for the needs of my department"

—TOWARD—

"I can influence solutions that benefit the entire organization."

7

A VIEW FROM THE BALCONY

No one person or perspective can give us
the answers we need to the problems of today.
Paradoxically, we can only find those answers
by admitting we don't know. We have to be
willing to let go of our certainty and expect
ourselves to be confused for a time. . . .
Yet I believe we will succeed in changing
this world only if we can think and work
together in new ways. Curiosity is what we need.
We don't have to let go of what we believe,
but we do need to be curious about what
someone else believes.

—MARGARET WHEATLEY
Turning to One Another

MEG WAS ON THE PHONE with me, grousing about issues she
kept running into between her department and the central office
of her law firm. I'd heard the rap a few times now. Her peer in
contracts was located in the home office and she in the field, where
the customers were—where the real action was happening as far

as Meg was concerned—and that peer was constantly putting road-blocks in her way and making things more difficult for her team.

"I get no respect from headquarters."

"They won't adopt any of my ideas."

"Every time I call, all they seem to do is question what we're doing. I never get to communicate with the executive team direct-ly. I always have to go through my division contacts. I swear they have it out for me."

Over the months I'd worked with her, I learned that Meg was bright, articulate, and capable, and she truly cared about doing what was right. She cared so much that she'd begun to stew over setbacks to the degree she was starting to sound paranoid. What was the problem? Were people in the home office corrupt, incom-petent, or maybe they just didn't like her? Was she being excluded from important impromptu meetings on purpose, or did people just not think about her when they scheduled them? She had expressed her displeasure repeatedly and pointedly and still received only resistance and rebuff.

"Doesn't the staff at headquarters care about what really matters?"

"How could they be so blind?"

"Is contracts withholding information and undermining com-munication with the customers *on purpose*?"

"Are they just clueless, or are they trying to make me look bad?"

Her complaints went on and on. She felt like a victim—*her biggest challenges and roadblocks all existed somewhere else.* The stress and anger were eating away at her personally and turning a job she'd once loved into a nightmare.

Maybe, I thought, *it's time to get a different perspective on things.*

Looking through a Different Lens

As coaches, we hear a lot about the problems and challenges that people experience. We use those issues as indicators of the work that needs to be done. The work usually involves initial awareness shifts so that our client has a broader view of the playing field and can create more options for how to respond to what they're experiencing. More options lead to changes in behaviors—which result in an increased ability to have a positive impact on the situations and people around them. Coaching helps leaders elevate and expand their perspective, as well as illuminate the blind spots that prevent good people from seeing how they are contributing to their own problems.

Even if others have actually wronged us or are really out to get us, we still get to choose our response. If we never stop to reflect and direct our thoughts in useful ways, we remain stuck—trapped in our well-rehearsed (but ineffective) thought patterns about what others are doing to mess with us. But we tend to need outside help to see beyond our habitual thought patterns—our own small picture of what's happening—and be opened up to viewing our situation from different viewpoints and perspectives.

Being open to positive ways to influence a situation is often an act of tremendous courage because it involves taking responsibility instead of blaming others. There is courage in being willing to look at how *we* are contributing to a troubling dynamic. It means

> *If we never stop to reflect and direct our thoughts in useful ways, we remain stuck—trapped in our well-rehearsed (but ineffective) thought patterns about what others are doing to mess with us.*

rejecting mistrustful and borderline paranoid speculation that those in charge "have it in for us." In Meg's case, her repeated refrain of "woe is me" needed to turn a corner before anything constructive was going to happen.

Meg put tremendous energy into advocating for her department's needs and interests while ignoring the bigger picture of the rest of the business, how her team's performance related to the overall organization, and the priorities of other departments to which her team contributed. I was not surprised that she was getting only grudging support from certain people at headquarters while many others outright ignored her and pursued their own priorities instead. It seemed that when they thought of Meg, it was more as a distraction and an irritant than a positive force helping move their agenda forward.

That put her in a difficult position to be influential. She felt marginalized, and her approach to addressing the situation was furthering the distance between her team and the home office. It was also clear that her role in the rift was not apparent to her, so she felt quite justified in her "truth" that others were at fault.

> "When we are motivated by a mission and we increase our awareness, we can learn what is needed and do what is required, even when it is hard."

It wasn't easy to shift Meg from the mindset that her role was to convince others how badly her team needed things—an "us versus them, and there's only so much to go around" mentality—to something more productive. Meg had a strong background in social justice, and the approach she was using now was the same one that had helped propel her to become a team lead at a young age. It felt right to Meg to be an advocate for her team and clients. Others *should* be willing to do whatever was necessary to support her causes. To move forward, however, Meg needed a better view of how her organization functioned to meet those objectives.

Seeing the Whole Dance Floor

To be effective, we need to see things as they really are, and see ourselves within the context of the grander scheme. As Ronald Heifetz writes in his book *Leadership Without Easy Answers*:

> Consider the experience of dancing on a dance floor in contrast with standing on a balcony and watching other people dance. Engaged in the dance, it is nearly impossible to get a sense of the patterns made by everyone on the floor. . . . To discern the larger patterns on the dance floor—to see who is dancing with whom, in what groups, in what location, and who is sitting out which kind of dance—we have to stop and get to the balcony.[11]

"Getting to the balcony" is a way to help yourself mentally take a step back and look at the whole picture. Being able to do so raises our awareness of what is going on in the system around us. This is really useful data, especially if we are trying to change that system.

When we are motivated by a mission and we increase our awareness, we can learn what is needed and do what is required, even when it is hard—even when it's different from our past behavior. We can choose and change. Our good character and principles shine through in these moments, because we put the big picture of what matters above our individual sense of comfort. Our honorable desire to serve wins out over lesser emotions. We allow ourselves to seek new perspectives to help us understand what is required to fulfill what we care about; defending against this awareness keeps us stuck.

Many people won't make this perspective change in their thinking, but it is available to anyone with an imagination. For instance, an executive—someone whose responsibility is the organization as a whole—has certain concerns, fears, and priorities that almost anyone can imagine if they try. Adopting a broader mindset—thinking from the perspective of a CEO, department chair, or board chairperson—is useful whether you aspire to be an executive or you need influence at that level, because it lets you step into a more holistic point of view. When you see the whole landscape and the interconnectedness of it—and see the one part you are involved with as a single piece of a larger whole—suddenly what you need to be doing to make progress becomes much clearer, and you can see the valuable linkages you can bring to the table. You become an advocate for what is best for the enterprise and its mission. When you do that, you'd be surprised how many more people want to hear what you have to say.

Meg had to admit that the pain of continuing to work the same way far outweighed the pain of experimenting with a broader perspective. She had been struggling to figure out a better way to work on her own—and there was so much to gain if things could be improved. Over time, Meg was able to develop sound strategies to address the underlying issues as she tried new ways of managing herself, her communications, and her projects. Her rate of learning accelerated when she saw how much change was possible. She simply started with the things she *could* control and stopped trying to overmanage the things she couldn't.

Getting a broader picture of her place in the dance helped Meg escape the downward spiral she was stuck in. As she moved onto the balcony, she could better see how issues were arising and how she was affecting others. With this understanding, she was better able to choreograph what was happening "on the floor" to create a thriving organization for the long term.

Viewed from the Whole, Priorities Change

Meg certainly needed to step back and see things from a broader viewpoint. This was not just about her and her team's feelings and preferences. They were a vital part of the overall organization, and they served a purpose beyond what she and her remote office did—and both needed each other to achieve better results. Starting to address issues from this broader perspective, and an outward mindset of what others needed from her rather than what she was trying to get from them,[12] soon gave her a new voice of influence with the home office.

Meg started asking for feedback that previously she had blocked. She experimented with new ways to meet the needs of her internal customers and collaborated to help them get the customers' voice from the field into decisions at headquarters. She even made a "highlights reel" from her visits to different locations to directly showcase the opportunities, challenges, and accolades from the customers' perspective. She took special delight when the annual report included insights that came from her work to build a bridge between the decision makers and "where the action was" in the field. She and her team built stronger relationships and delivered consistent value to the overall organization.

The shift for Meg was, in a very real sense, a matter of growing into her potential to expand her awareness and see outside herself, one added perspective at a time. Each time she took an issue that previously she would have seen as an injustice to her team, she purposefully looked at it from a different, less internally focused lens. There were many layers to her work, including her relationships with the headquarters staff, policies, communication channels, and the structure of the service offerings. On each one, she could make real progress by working from a broader perspective that included others' viewpoints. She found this more effectively enabled her to effect change rather than simply advocating about what was "right" based on her own team's interests. This expansion of thinking and expanded influence brought a new sense of empowerment and purpose in everything she did.

WHY Do the Reflection Exercises?

» To increase your influence and the impact of what you do.

» To transition from protecting individual interests to advocating for what is best for the whole.

» So you can propose solutions that are recognized as valuable.

» In order to build your personal compassion for and connection to the issues experienced by others in your organization.

REFLECTION EXERCISES

1. Consider the last thirty days at your office. Where have you been trying to be heard?

2. Next, pick one example where you were trying to be heard. Imagine a future where your influence created the change you seek. Describe what it would look like.

3. Consider a perspective held by a leader in your work world who you don't understand, appreciate, or agree with. While it may be uncomfortable to consider their viewpoint, give it a try. *What would be important to a person who held that perspective?*

4. If you held this leader's responsibilities, what would you be most worried about? Can you reframe his or her perspective in a constructive light, even though you disagree with it?

5. What, if anything, do you and this leader both care about? Is there any common purpose? What is the whole of which you are both an important part?

6. Is there a way to further what you both care about by incorporating some of both of your perspectives? How can you communicate in a way that includes the broader view in order to be more fully heard?

THE SHIFT:

—FROM—

"Work more efficiently"

—TOWARD—

"Act more strategically."

THE FREEDOM TO INITIATE

> When you look at strategy as a
> frame of mind to be cultivated, rather than
> as a plan to be executed, you are far more
> likely to succeed over the long run.

—CYNTHIA MONTGOMERY
author of *The Strategist: Be the Leader Your Business Needs*
and former chair of the strategy unit at Harvard Business School

AS A NEW TEAM LEAD, Larry wanted to show those who reported to him, his boss, and himself that he could rock his new role. The environment at his organization was very task-oriented, and many on his team had been in their jobs for years. The work was routine, and there was always more that needed to be done than there was time to do it. There was a ton of backlog and new demands from all sides. Most of the group dealt with the pressure-cooker environment by keeping their heads down and focusing on the day-to-day. They were afraid that if they looked up they would see that the light at the end of the tunnel was really an oncoming train.

Larry felt responsible to provide perspective and direction to help people look up, out, and across to manage their work more effectively. He had a gut instinct that there had to be a way to take control of their workloads and not just keep plodding on the path of least resistance, even though he wasn't sure what it was.

Compounding his intuition, his manager was new to the organization and had some pretty assertive ideas herself. She made it clear she expected Larry to step up, own his leadership role, and be willing to take risks that could lead to mistakes. *She wants me to make mistakes?* That threw him for a loop. Talk about jumping into the deep end! Transitioning from the bureaucratic, heads-down, protective environment Larry had come from to leading the way as a risk-taking innovator was going take some serious mindset and skillset changes.

Fortunately, Larry was glad to stretch out of his comfort zone to test his limits and those of his team members. Even though it was nerve-racking, he was willing to push through the fear and try some new ways of doing. At the same time, Larry liked the details of the work and worried that he gravitated too much into the weeds when talking with his manager. So when she asked him if he would like to work with a management coach, he agreed. He thought it might open him up to new possibilities. As his coach, I was able to support him as he stretched into new territory.

Larry went to work on assessing the environment for opportunities, building relationships, tackling challenges, making decisions, and exploring how to work with me. He hoped to leverage his fellow team leads as resources for figuring out what to do and to help him accomplish something that would benefit the whole company. There were twelve other team leads in the department, and Larry was looking forward to feeling greater camaraderie and acceptance from them as a peer.

Engaging the Power of Strategy

Strategic thinkers use everyday events as launching points to imagine what could happen when variables are shifted. As we discussed before, Einstein's thought experiments provide a great example of the power of one's mind to consider alternate futures, learn from these extrapolations, and apply data to current concerns. With dynamic variables such as advancing technology, climate change, politics, economic fluctuations, and human nature, change is inevitable and constant. But how will those changes impact you and your organization, in which directions, and when? Seeing where you fit in context to these factors seeds a strategic perspective. What's your best path forward? What are your biggest risks? Where are the opportunities? Where are the bottlenecks? Coming up with options to navigate this kind of complexity is what strategy is all about.

Strategy illuminates priorities through logic and insight—if this is the desired end goal, then these are the actions with the best potential to lead us there. Those who are strategic about their daily work maintain a focus on short-term tactics inside a context of long-term goals. Bit by bit, they line up their actions to shape and reshape ideas, departments, organizations, and industries.[13] Alignment with strategic priorities is the source of the freedom to initiate.

Part of Larry's quest, although he may not have been able to articulate it yet, was to position himself for the future of his organization and his career. New capabilities in technology, new types of complex problems, and increased digitization and mobilization would undoubtedly one day be mainstream. Will he have the capabilities needed to keep up with these changes and utilize them effectively?

Larry's manager asked that he focus on issues linked to their strategic priorities, ask for what he needed, and keep her informed about progress and problems. She wanted him to take hold of his freedom to initiate, but also to keep alignment with her and the existing priorities. She didn't want Larry working on "gravity" problems—the type of issues that are impervious to change. She wanted him to impact the financial bottom line: to retain and retrain the staff to be more efficient and prepared for the demands on the horizon. This was a different way of managing than Larry had experienced. Previously, his managers had been more directive and interested in him implementing *their* ideas. None had ever encouraged him to initiate his own ideas or ever really referenced strategic priorities.

When Strategic Thinking Meets Everyday Problems

In his next team meeting, Larry had one of his staff members describe a problem she was having, while another shared what he had done to solve it. As they spoke, Larry saw the opportunity to create a template to help replicate the results, and perhaps eventually automate it. This could be the type of solution his boss was looking for. By creating an easier way to do the work, it corrected the problem, and it would free up time. As a result, individual customers could each get a little more mindshare.

Larry saw this could have upsides for his team and their customers. And it was a way to show his manager he was taking initiative in a useful way. He had several more conversations with his team to map out what they could do to address the problem through an automated process, including real-time reporting and creating a database of shared responses.

He presented the idea to the other team leads and asked them for feedback. When they agreed the template would help them as well, Larry went back to his manager and described the result that his team members had achieved and how it benefited others who were facing similar problems. Then he requested resources to help create a more robust solution template that they could share across the department. Larry explained how the model could help them anticipate needs more broadly. His manager nodded encouragingly as he shared his thoughts and delineated the solution template's potential to improve their metrics.

Larry could have made other choices. He could have decided it was not his problem and done nothing about it. He could have asked others to set up a committee to discuss it. He could have researched beyond his organization to find out how other groups dealt with it. He could have gone ahead with the initiative and never consulted his manager. He could have criticized a different department for causing the problem his staff was experiencing. Literally hundreds of options exist for how to deal with a persistent problem, some potentially resulting in significantly more value than others to the team, the person, and the organization.

As the templates he'd created came online six months later, Larry was glad his first initiative worked out well. He began looking for others in the organization who were operating in this way, hoping to amplify their efforts.

Adopting a Strategic Mindset

When looking for evidence of strategic thinking to create value, you may notice the following three interlocking signs: a future orientation, a big-picture view, and a curiosity about ways to create value.

1. A Future Orientation

Since the future hasn't happened yet, we can only guess at how it will turn out. Rather than expecting the past to be a predictor of what will happen next or trying to convince ourselves or others that we "know" how things will unfold, strategic thinkers look for the drivers that will impact future outcomes. Visualizing numerous scenarios and considering how you would respond in each creates more options when it comes time to decide what you actually *will* do.

Instead of thinking only about how to minimize risk or what could go wrong, look for a game you can win—something with an upside for what you care about.

Projecting forward in time to imagine what could go wrong is useful as well, but it has limits. Driving yourself nuts worrying about bad things that *could* happen can make you feel awful. Plenty of people create anxiety for themselves in this way without adding any value. Sometimes people even have an unreasonable attachment to the negative futures they predict, not because they are more likely to happen, but because they came up with them. Even though they don't want a particular event to come to pass, sometimes they will unconsciously undermine what is best for the organization just for the thrill of being proven "right" about how bad they said things could get.

Instead of thinking only about how to minimize risk or what could go wrong, look for a game you can win—something with an upside for what you care about. If you are needing inspiration for better options, you may want to look at upsides and successes created in other industries or organizations. You are looking for what else you would want to see flourish in the future so that you can plant those seeds now.

2. Taking the Big-Picture View

It takes effort to look beyond one's own part and see a broader view of the context and circumstances that encompass the whole, including people who see the situation differently. *Strategic thinkers try on a big-picture view of the situation, and then stretch to an even bigger picture by looking at what is impacting the circumstances they are in.*

The ability to see across the whole allows you to see more interconnections and more sides to the story. You may have missed part of the picture simply based on the volume and variety of information available to take in, or because of the limited perspective of the particular job or department you work in. A systems view prompts deeper insights and greater wisdom about what may unfold overall. One more reason to climb up to the balcony so you can see the entire dance floor.

3. Curious about Ways to Create Value

Those who are interested in growing their capability demonstrate curiosity about how to make a difference. They ask questions to help them understand more. They are open to out-of-the-box ideas. They see current experiences as building new learning for the future. They're not afraid of trial and error, especially if the cost of failure is low.

Having a growth mindset (as we discussed in Chapter Three) that is eager to learn drives behaviors that create access to more, better, and broader sources of information and application. Curiosity loves problem solving, investigating, experimenting, asking questions, and learning from others. A growth mindset—or "a learning framework"—results in greater persistence and the ability to build new skills. Conversely, a fixed mindset focuses on how to be successful only with what already exists. A "knower" reacts defensively when challenged with another point of view; a "learner" is willing to take calculated risks for the sake of potential gains. If you are looking to create value and make a positive difference in your organization, you'll want to be an agile learner rather than a defensive knower.

Meet the Future Strategically Rather than Reactively

These three perspectives are common among those who shape valuable new initiatives. You won't talk with a strategic thinker for very long about their process before you hear all three come out. Accomplished strategic leaders deliberately think through scenarios about the future, notice the bigger picture, and learn along the way, engaging others and investigating possibilities. These are exactly the same mindsets and tools Larry began developing to better lead his team and make strategic improvements for his organization.

WHY Do the Reflection Exercises?

» So you can engage in strategic thinking from the perspective of your current role.

» To identify ways you can initiate new ideas that align with strategic priorities.

» In order to amplify the impact of your efforts.

» To inspire curiosity about how to create more value.

REFLECTION EXERCISES

1. In a couple of sentences, how would you describe a present issue, problem, or opportunity to someone who does not work in your industry?

2. Consider your purpose, mission, or prior plans. How does this situation create an opportunity to further a larger goal? What would make this situation really useful to you? How good could it get?

3. What are the key choices at stake? What are the deciding factors that will influence how this turns out?

4) Create alternative scenarios for the future of your organization or for your career. Extrapolate and use your imagination to get at a vivid level of detail about both positive and negative potential outcomes.

   a. What stories would you like to be telling about this future?
   b. What might happen that is great?
   c. What might you want to avoid?
   d. What decisions and actions could influence each of those outcomes?
   e. What combination of choices might get you closer to the story you would like to be able to tell?

5. Do you have enough options? Create more distinct opportunities by looking at the situation from different perspectives.

   a. What would be a bolder option?
   b. What would be less risky?
   c. What could accomplish things more quickly?
   d. What could you leverage that already exists?
   e. What would make it even more likely to work out well?
   f. Is it feasible in both the short-term and long-term?
   g. What other ways are there to look at this?

6. What can you do to start moving forward this week?

THE SHIFT:

—FROM—

"I'm doing the best I can"

—TOWARD—

"I'm curious and open to learning new things about myself and others."

9

ILLUMINATING BLIND SPOTS

To grow and flourish, you need accurate
information about how your behavior impacts
others—how you're perceived and experienced by
those with whom you live and work. Armed with
good-quality information, you can make wise,
informed decisions about repeating behaviors
that support your success and choosing new
behaviors where change is warranted.

—TERESSA MOORE GRIFFIN
founder and CEO of Spirit of Purpose

AS THE LONGTIME executive director of an underfunded
community center, Allison was running from one issue to another,
usually feeling like her hair was on fire. She was trying, unsuccessfully, to keep her spirits up. There was always so much to do.
She loved the organization and what it stood for. She longed for
it to achieve the success, stability, and recognition it could and
should. She loved the community members whom she saw regularly. She felt their programs and instructors were innovative, and
they helped people around them get more out of their lives and

live with more meaning. The organization was financially solvent enough to keep their programs going, pay their too-small staff on time if not generously, and keep their facility presentable, even if it required a bit of finagling and ingenuity to avoid bottoming out before the end of each fiscal year. (Thankfully, they had a number of generous supporters who also believed in the value of what they did.)

Allison had been with the organization for twelve years, but it still felt like they were running—or rather, trying to build—a start-up. The community center lacked basic infrastructure in key areas, such as a formal business model, and they desperately needed systems to streamline administration. But who had time to stop and do that when there were so many urgent day-to-day matters demanding immediate attention?

Pulled in many directions, Allison was also feeling criticized on all sides. No one understood the whole of what she dealt with on a daily basis, and each person seemed to think she should devote more time or create better results in whatever area they cared about the most. Between the lack of staff capacity, the workload, and the unbelievable number of activities going on, her current job was not sustainable, even though, somehow, she managed. The demands grew each year, and it was slowly affecting her health—another thing she was in denial about. One person can do only so much.

Then, to top it all off, she was told that a 360-degree feedback process was going to be put in place so she could hear the opinions of those who worked with her.

Great! she thought. *Not like I don't get enough "feedback" already!*

The more she heard about the process, the more it filled her with dread. She figured this would open her up to more criticism on what she wasn't accomplishing. She knew there was really no way to meet everyone's expectations, so it felt like this was simply an excuse to call her on the carpet to account for her failures.

The feedback would tell her about how her work was going, what her strengths were (as perceived by others), as well as areas where she could improve. She would also learn about how people felt about changes that were happening and about any gaps in communications she could close. The consultants told her the feedback would help her know how her work impacted others, etc., etc. The more they told her about it, the more she felt like it was a setup. Maybe they were just looking for an excuse to replace her. The thought made her shudder and then laugh. Maybe it would be a good thing all around. She was fed up. Something needed to change, and even getting replaced might be a good thing.

The feedback was collected, and the night before her meeting with the consultants, they sent her the report so she could review it. Although Allison had been through many performance reviews, she'd never been through a process like this. It felt intensely personal. So much of the discussion was about her, and so many of the people in her community had shared their impressions.

As she read through the reactions, her anxiety rose. One comment really stuck with her:

> Allison has a servant's heart, and she always wants to make sure everyone is getting what they need. That's great, but she's also the director of the center. Sometimes it doesn't feel like she's as proactive or organized as she should be; like she doesn't have the confidence she should, given what she knows.

Another comment:

> *Allison is very good at fixing things on the fly, but some of the problems we face feel more systemic. If she put some policies or directives in place instead of making temporary work-arounds, I can think of many things that would run more smoothly and be less of a headache for everyone, including her.*

Her first reaction was *Ouch!* All that stood out were criticisms of the way she organized things and what she did. That hurt. She wasn't sure if it was true, but she also wasn't sure it wasn't. She couldn't help but let the tears roll down as she thought about it. Didn't they understand how hard she was working just to keep things afloat?

After letting the initial sting subside, though, she went back and found the section under "Strengths" and started re-reading. *Did they have anything nice to say?* Several people complimented her on her commitment, on how many hours she put in, on how much she cared, and about how she treated everyone with such respect. One said, "You can really tell she cares about the programs and that everyone is enjoying their classes." Someone else called her "the glue that held the center together."

That felt good.

Then she read another:

> *Allison, sometimes I think you have no understanding of how much people around here look up to you and appreciate what you do—or that we'd actually benefit from hearing more about what you think. You're always so interested in how we've grown, but how are you growing? Sometimes people worry that you're working yourself to death.*

That made her wonder, *How am I growing?*

She decided to put the papers away and wait to meet with the consultants before digging any deeper.

The next morning, when the consultants asked her about her initial reactions to the feedback, Allison explained it was nice to get some positive feedback, but that some of it had hurt. She wasn't sure some of the criticisms were fair.

The consultants nodded, and then waited for her to continue.

"I feel like I'm trying to catch up most of the time," she confided. "Then something happens I need to fix, and it puts me even further behind. By the end of the day, I feel just that much further behind."

Again they nodded.

Allison looked down at the report on the table before her and collected her thoughts, remembering some of the comments. "I'd certainly like things to be different," she eventually went on to fill the silence. "But most of these suggestions seem impossible, given what I deal with on a day-to-day basis."

"*Most* of them?" one of the consultants asked.

"Yes," she affirmed.

"Well, then, which ones don't?" the other asked.

She looked back down at the report, lifted the top page, and started looking through the feedback again. "Well, like this one about organizing the main office a little better so everything had a place and it could be tidied up more easily. That's a good suggestion. I'd never thought of it as a problem, but I can see how it could help."

Again the consultants nodded, giving her room to go on.

Over the next hour or so, she picked through what people had written, considering each suggestion, criticism, and commendation. The consultants asked a lot of questions as she considered each response. Quite often, when she noted something that hurt her feelings or identified what she saw as unrealistic, they would see it differently. In fact, they often found something positive in it. They helped her see the difference between her intention—where she was coming from and what she was trying to accomplish for others—and the experience others were having. They helped her see that if she is getting information only from her own point of view, she probably didn't have the data she needed.

As she slowly opened herself up to the feedback and suggestions, she began to see some things she thought she could improve and recognized some attitudes that had been holding her back. By the time they were done, she no longer saw the report as being overly critical, but rather affirming of who she was and of her capability to direct the facility and its programs. At the same time, she also got a glimpse of some habits, attitudes, and practices she would be better off without. By the end of the two hours (which flew by incredibly quickly), she saw three main areas of action she could start working on in the short-term:

1. Allison decided to entrust her teachers and volunteers with handling more of the daily tasks—and some of the emergencies—even when she felt shorthanded. This would give her time to think about more systematic and strategic solutions.

2. She would start preparing her Executive Director's Report in advance of board meetings rather than the day of. This would help her determine the main points beforehand, find a more positive way to express them, and help her have a forward focus.

3. One of the classes at the center was in home organization and decluttering, so she asked the teacher if she

would spend an hour with her in the main offices and give her some tips. Together, they established systems to make the office more efficient and keep it habitually neater.

Over the next six months, making incremental improvements in each of these areas had a cumulatively positive effect, creating more order in her physical environment, greater clarity of communication, and an increased ability for Allison to focus on strategic goals for the center while others tackled the day-to-day. That gave her more time to think at a higher level across multiple projects. As a result, she was able to do more to support the volunteers and committee members working on the detailed tasks that used to eat up so much of her time and energy.

Allison later told me that meeting with those consultants changed her life. By the end of that year, the whole organization had changed with her. She felt more in control, more like she was leading her responsibilities rather than running behind them. She had more energy and appreciation for her work, the organization, and their progress. Of course, running a community center in a fragile economy was still challenging, but she loved her township and had found ways to increase her contribution to it. The satisfaction she drew from serving her purpose renewed her energy and strengthened her resolve to keep learning.

Participating in Your Journey

Mission-driven professionals like Allison care about others and want to help them. Since feedback provides data on how you are impacting others, it is supremely useful when you desire to know whether your efforts are having the intended effect. Originally, feedback was a military tool that provided data about whether a cannon shot was on target. Imagine trying to figure out if you had aimed correctly and hit the target if you couldn't see where the cannonball landed. You would need someone else to tell you where it landed relative to the target. In my mind, I imagine a helpful person saying, "A little to the left" or "That hits the mark" when I receive feedback. This helps me remember that even if it hurts to hear it, I need the information to know how to adjust so I can get closer to my intended goal.

People tend not to view themselves accurately or objectively—and may genuinely not be aware of how their behavior and choices impact others. If you are listening only to yourself, you're probably not getting the whole story. Feedback helps us know how close we are to hitting the mark of our intention. Feedback is particularly useful for leaders because greater self-awareness results in a closer match between intention and impact. Because we prefer to judge ourselves on our intentions rather than our impact, sometimes the feedback we receive is not what we want to hear. Illuminating the gap between our intention and our impact is the gift of feedback, and we can learn to appreciate its value. Then we get to decide how, or if, we will shift.

If you are listening only to yourself, you're probably not getting the whole story.

Stopping to evaluate—and feedback like Allison received is a great evaluation tool—allows us to recognize others' perspectives and be more intentional about our choices. This data prompts awareness that gives us more control over our own lives and careers. This can make all the difference in getting more out of the life and work we love.

WHY **Do the Reflection Exercises?**

» To distinguish the gap between your intention and your impact.

» To be able to use feedback productively, even when it hurts.

» So you can feel more in control and proactive about making needed changes.

» To raise your awareness by seeing the perspectives of others.

REFLECTION EXERCISES

1. List three to five people whom you would trust to give you feedback on your work and might have ideas for how you could get better at what you do.

2. In what areas do you feel "stuck" in a way of doing things that isn't really working? What have you tried to do to address it? Have you asked for feedback from others about this?

3. When people give you suggestions, how do you react? Do you feel they are attacking you or criticizing you? Why do you think you feel as you do?

4. How would you create an environment for receiving feedback that would work best for you? (Would you do it in person? Have them fill out a questionnaire? Maybe do it through a third party?)

5. When you receive feedback that is at odds with your understanding, how do you reconcile the differences?

6. Can you be true to yourself and be open to receiving feedback at the same time? How can you allow other people's viewpoints to positively impact your growth?

THE SHIFT:

—FROM—

"Disengaged and disappointed"

—TOWARD—

"Shaping my future and adding value to my company."

10

INTERSECTING OBJECTIVES

Who you are, what your values are,
what you stand for—they are your anchor,
your north star. You won't find them in a book.
You'll find them in your soul.

—ANNE M. MULCAHY
former chairperson and CEO of Xerox Corporation

BETH WAS A NEW MANAGER with a programmer on her team, Howard, who just wouldn't take ownership for his work, his place on the team, or the requirements of his role. She felt as though she had tried everything and was frustrated, without a clue what to do. The situation didn't look good for Howard. The current path pointed toward a performance improvement plan, a painful process of documenting his shortcomings, all eventually leading to his termination. This was not the outcome Beth wanted. So she asked me about finding a way to engage him in some honest problem solving before going down the justifying-his-termination route.

It started with a simple question. I told her, "Ask him what he's really interested in." We theorized that if she could understand what Howard *did* care about and inspired more engagement in him, maybe she could pair his interests with things his role required and the two could feed each other.

It was rocky at first. She had to develop trust—to build a relationship that was positive and open. This hadn't been her experience with Howard. He was introverted and not very communicative. He avoided eye contact and was frequently late to the office. She noticed he had a lot of childcare issues, which he often used as excuses for not stepping up. It turned out he'd become a father at a young age, his wife had left him alone with the child, and he didn't have any extended family in the area. As a result, he always seemed in a rush and disheveled. His hygiene was also inconsistent. Some days, just being in his presence was a struggle.

After a couple of attempts at conversation, Howard finally shared that he hoped one day to be a professor. He imagined himself at a college teaching physics or another scientific discipline. His current job as a programmer for a database system wasn't much like that. No wonder he was disengaged. As they explored his aspirations, Beth started asking prompting questions that helped him trace back from his long-range goals: "What skills would you need to be a great professor?"

Howard thought he would need to be comfortable with speaking in front of a group and be able to organize "lessons" to convey complex concepts to students in a way they could understand. He would need to master the content so he felt prepared to teach and comfortable with being questioned. Beth began looking for how he might garner some of that preparation in his current job. Her goal was to find a way to engage him and help him take responsibility.

The company had periodic interdisciplinary education sessions where peers shared what they were learning and kept each other apprised of innovations or emerging practices that could be spread to other parts of the organization. This seemed like a perfect spot for Beth to encourage Howard to "test out" being a professor. But what was Howard doing that would be worth sharing with his colleagues?

In their next conversation, she asked Howard if there was any aspect of his work that he thought others would benefit from. Was there anything he was doing differently from his peers that was working well? He'd never been asked a question like this before. Most peers just asked about things he wasn't doing. At first he was shy to admit it, but he had built a library of routines to make the programming easier, faster, and more consistent. He thought that others might be able to tap into the same library and save some time if they knew about it.

Beth was pleased, but also a little nervous about asking Howard to present his routines. No one had authorized him to build a library, but she arranged for him to organize a presentation on how the library worked and about the routines he used most often. She had him practice the presentation on his own and then in front of her in an empty conference room. She helped him make it more interactive, visual, and concrete. She watched his progress and coached him on speaking more clearly and confidently, as well as on how to project his voice so everyone in the room could hear him.

Beth reported to me that in the series of conversations leading up to his presentation, Howard started looking her in the eye, was more frequently on time, and with a little nudging and some praise for his progress, he also began to pay more attention to his appearance.

What do you think was the impact of Howard's developmental experience?

Beth shared that it was highly motivational to both of them. Getting interested in Howard's personal objectives, and then helping him make the most of what he was contributing, was the best lever she could find to move him toward being an engaged, valuable employee. It felt like a real win-win. His self-directed learning and experience implementing a new approach became an asset to the company, and she saved herself from the painful process of laying Howard off and finding and training a new employee.

Over time, Beth became a highly effective manager by finding the intersection between personal and organizational objectives for those on her team. Leaders like Beth, who inspire, challenge, and connect with people's motivations find their employees take on more responsibility. They also feel greater loyalty to the company, and they deepen their contribution and commitment. The high performance that results benefits those team members with career advancement, development opportunities, new skills, and greater capabilities as they move forward. For Beth, she found new joy as a manager who helped others cash in their Third Paycheck.

Where Your Aspirations Meet the Organization's Needs

To find the points where your aspirations and skill development mesh with your company's needs, look first to the strategic direction and objectives of your department or function.* Use the following guidelines to identify the strategies of your organization that are relevant to your role and to determine how to help advance

---

* That many employees have to work hard to figure out their organization's strategic vision still amazes me. Companies say they want aligned, engaged employees, but at the same time they frequently make it hard for employees to know what their strategic direction is, much less how that direction relates to specific jobs within the organization. Organizations *shouldn't* make this hard for you to discover if they want you to care about it, but sometimes they spend so much time thinking about their goals that it never occurs to them that no one else in their company knows what they are. (If you are a manager, now is a good time to consider whether or not those who report to you know the organization's priorities. Are you sure they do?)

company objectives *while* you move toward your desired future, building the skillsets and mindsets you'll need along the way.

1. Identify Organizational Objectives

What are your organization's needs? Write your answer to this question so you can refer to it and update it as your understanding increases and as circumstances change. (This is another good reason for having a journal.) Then investigate what you are being told by your organization and supervisors about what you are all aiming to accomplish. (When you start tracking your organization's strategic goals, you are already developing a capability many of your colleagues are not.) Select the questions below that apply to your situation and gather the information:

» What does the strategic plan say are the key goals, objectives, or challenges for this year?

» If there is no apparent strategic plan, what do you see as the key issues facing the organization?

» How would you describe what is important to the company and your manager overall? (This is not a time to be snarky or cynical—"jerking people around" and "micromanaging" are not helpful answers here, even if they are the unintended impact of manager behavior. Go upstream to figure out what they are really trying to accomplish and plug into that instead.)

» What are the stated goals for your department or division?

» If there are no clear goals, then what is appreciated or rewarded, or seems to be expected?

» What do people in leadership talk about at meetings or company communications?

You might also ask your manager what your department is being evaluated on this year. Metrics reveal what an organization is focused on. Budgets do too. If you know what is and is not being funded, you have some indication of the priorities.

Based on this information, you may want to extend your research to other organizations in your industry or sector. Pay attention to trends that are in the news or shifts in technology or other factors that may shape the future of your organization. If you haven't been with the organization for very long, ask a longer-term employee about the shifts in strategy for the organization over time.

2. Your Interests for Your Future

As Beth asked Howard, ask yourself what you are really interested in long-term—not necessarily related to this job or position only, but more broadly. You are looking for aspirations that you can start building toward. Consider journaling or typing up your responses to any of these questions that apply:

> » What assignments would you want to do, even if no one was paying you?
>
> » What brings you joy when you work on it?
>
> » What do you want out of your career?
>
> » Where do you want to be of service?
>
> » If you could add value to the organization in any area, what would you want to do?
>
> » What skills are most interesting to you or pertinent to your growth?
>
> » What are the gaps in your knowledge or experience?

Based on this information, start to notice what you desire to get better at. Leadership qualities, such as the ability to inspire others to action, facilitation skills, technology skills, financial acumen, and synthesizing data from multiple sources are all examples of skills entrepreneurs need. If you dream of starting your own business or social enterprise someday, what would it take for you to be effective? What capabilities do you need? If you don't know what skills are needed, look at the careers of people who have been effective doing what you want to do and see what skills, approaches, and mindsets they have. If you can, find primary sources where they are telling their stories: online interviews or their blog, biographies of their lives (especially autobiographies), magazine articles on them, etc. Build your list and prioritize the top five capabilities you wish to work on first.

3. Opportunities at the Intersections

Next, consider multiple options for how you might make connections between the list of organizational priorities and your interests. Use your creativity to invent or reinvent an aspect of your role or create a project that can encompass both the needs of your organization and your passions. If it is not possible to find a fitting project within the organization, this would be a great time to investigate the potential for a pro bono community project that you could design and volunteer to lead. There are always groups that can benefit from a volunteer who wants to learn while providing free support to a nonprofit organization, school, faith-based group, or government initiative.

This project may be something you spend only an hour a week on, or it could be much more, but the joy and challenge it brings will radiate to enhance your whole work/life experience. In fact, many people find that a small project infused with their personal passion and excitement can initiate a career breakthrough. Having one project that "sings to your soul" can transform your life at work from a chore, or a bore, to a door leading somewhere you want to go.

Focus on What You Can Influence

You may remember author Stephen Covey's Circle of Influence, introduced in his book *The 7 Habits of Highly Effective People.* He wrote about the two circles that encompass things we care about and things we can do something about. The Circle of Concern connects to what we care about—from the personal concerns of our health, career, relationships, etc.—to the worldwide concerns of economic stability, climate change, war, food quality, etc. The Circle of Influence is the subset of our concerns that we can actually do something about: those areas where we can have an impact through our own actions. Covey shows the value of focusing proactively on the areas where we can have influence, because when we take action and do what we can do, we ignite change, create opportunities for our Circle of Influence, and impact growth.

WHY Do the Reflection Exercises?

» To link personal aspirations with organizational opportunities.

» In order to uncover your motivational drivers for growth.

» To design self-directed learning that works for you and your organization.

» To be more creative and generate better ideas for moving your career forward.

REFLECTION EXERCISES

1. What skills are required for the roles you would love to have in the future? List five of the highest priority skills.

2. Are you ready to plan a way to grow those skills, even if your organization or manager doesn't support it? Notice your emotional connection to being self-directed in your learning.

3. What would stoke your innate drive to learn and grow?

4. What possible ways could you start building the highest priority skills for your desired future? What would be a good starting point?

5. Who could be an ally or a supporter as you build new skills?

6. How (and where) can it be fun and easy to learn and grow while you work?

THE SHIFT:

—FROM—

"Mistakes are an indictment
of my abilities"

—TOWARD—

"Mistakes are to be
learned from and leveraged."

11

WRITE A GREAT LAST CHAPTER

> We are wrong about what it means
> to be wrong. Far from being a sign of intellectual
> inferiority, the capacity to err is crucial to
> human cognition.... Thanks to error,
> we can revise our understanding of ourselves
> and amend our ideas about the world.
>
> **—KATHRYN SCHULZ**
> Pulitzer Prize–winning journalist

JOHN DIDN'T WANT to admit it, but it was his fault the wrong document was sent. He was moving too fast and just trying to get it sent in time to catch his train. If he missed the train, there were consequences at home, so he left without double-checking the work, which screwed up their chances for the client renewal. This might cost him his job. Feeling trapped and sullen, John braced himself for the blamefest to come.

Sherri knew the moment she walked into her boss's office that she'd done something wrong. Seeing his stiff posture and lips pinched together, she just knew. It made her want to run, but she did the normal thing and took a seat. *What am I going to do if they fire me?* flashed through her mind. She'd just made a down payment on a house last week, and she couldn't imagine forfeiting it. *Maybe I should have stayed in my old job?* It was boring, but everyone thought she was great. Here they pick apart everything, and it's like you are already supposed to know. Her resentment rising, she thought, *They just don't tell me what I need to know until it's too late. And then they tell me I screwed up again and—* "Sherri, are you listening?" she heard from across the table. She looked up like a deer in headlights.

Rob left his second in command, Mary, in charge when he was assigned to a new division. He'd felt good about it. She had seen him manage all sorts of changes and challenges and had been a good thinking partner along the way. The reports from his old division became increasingly disturbing, however. He thought it would blow over, and they would get used to her. He decided to keep his distance so people would learn to rely on her. He stopped engaging with staff from the old division, except to say good-bye to the ones who left. As he did, he saw some of the best talent was walking out the door. He now realized he'd made a huge mistake by expecting Mary to carry forward what he had started. Reflecting, he realized that he'd never put her out in front to practice executive leadership and receive mentoring while he was there. He didn't really know how she would lead until he left, because she'd never had to lead when he was in charge. If only he could turn back the clock.

John, Sherri, and Rob provide three examples of mistakes that could derail progress—or could be opportunities to create better endings. Mistakes are emotionally charged, in part, because we like being right. We are afraid of tarnishing our image, and we don't want to do anything that would hurt the causes or people we care about. Conscientious people try to avoid making mistakes, but they still happen.

Solving problems defines much of business life. We see an issue, a risk, a snag in our plans, or an unexpected predicament created by someone's mistake or carelessness, and now it needs to be dealt with. *Who will get the blame? Who will lose face? Was it my fault?* We sometimes worry over these situations even years later. We even agonize over other people's mistakes: *How could they have thought that was a good idea? What were they thinking? Look at the mess they made!*

I know of no way to avoid mistakes entirely, especially if you are working toward an important personal and professional purpose and growing your skills along the way. As Margaret Heffernan, author of *Women on Top* and *A Bigger Prize*, put it: "If you have never failed at anything, then you haven't been trying hard enough, aren't very imaginative, or have had such extraordinarily good luck that you have come to believe you are invincible."

The other side of the coin is that, when doing something new or innovative, mistakes can be vital for breakthrough.

> Sometimes, what was originally considered a mistake opens up new possibilities that wouldn't have been possible without the original misstep.

There is value and learning to be gained in mistakes that we'd never realize if the mistakes hadn't happened. A more productive quest than avoiding mistakes is improving how we flow through mistakes—our own and those made by others—in order to gain new insights and make changes based on what we learn. Regardless of how large or small the mistake, we always have a choice about what we do next. Sometimes, what was originally considered a mistake opens up new possibilities that wouldn't have been possible without the original misstep.

According to a study from the Center for Creative Leadership, when leaders from a large sample of Fortune 500 companies were asked about the key events that contributed to their success, 34 percent of leaders said they learned the most from significant hardships, setbacks, and mistakes. This was the biggest source of learning identified! Greater than learning from others (22 percent), challenging assignments (27 percent), and all other learning events put together (17 percent).[14] Imagine cutting yourself off from all of this potential gain by never facing your mistakes head on!

On a developmental journey, mistakes can be very useful—*supremely* useful.

Coming to Terms with Mistakes

During hiring interviews at my firm, we ask people to talk about their strengths and accomplishments, but we also ask: "Despite our best efforts, we all make mistakes at times, and sometimes they can have large implications. Tell us about a time this happened to you."

The responses are incredibly revealing. I remember several candidates who could not recall any mistakes. They turned red as they remembered them internally, or perhaps they were simply embarrassed that they couldn't think of any. We felt them squirm. Without awareness of having made a mistake, there is no opportunity to turn one into something else. Not seeing a mistake is not the same as not having made it. These denials demonstrated a lack of self-awareness and lost potential for learning.

Most candidates we ask about their mistakes take a few minutes to reflect—you can watch them tilt their head back a bit, eyes roaming up or down to help them sort through their databanks to find a meaty and socially acceptable mistake to share. Once they identify a mistake, it is fascinating to watch their body language as they retell it. As an employer screening for new hires who will fit into our deliberately developmental culture, I am looking for a number of things:

» **Degree of ownership**: Do they see the part they played in the circumstance, or are they trying to shift the blame entirely to someone or something else?

» **Perspective**: Given that the mistake is from the past, and not something they are in right now, how are they affected by recalling it? Do they seem to be reliving it? Have they grown from it, learned something, or released or reduced the angst?

» **Growth mindset**: Do they have compassion for themselves and others in the situation for being imperfect and on a path of learning? Do they experience empathy for those who were negatively impacted? Is there an opening for learning in the future, or do they see it as an indictment of fixed capability?

» **Solution**: How did they address the actual circumstance? Did they fix it, rectifying the mistake? Or did they seek exoneration so no one would blame them?

» **Leverage**: Was there any positive byproduct created by the mistake? Perhaps it was a learning experience that has been integrated and now serves to prevent similar mistakes from happening. Perhaps their corrective action to address the mistake produced an innovation, or an evolution of a process, or a new way to handle issues of this type?

A person's internal wiring and orientation to mistakes is really helpful to know as an employer, and it is something that everyone can manage and improve for themselves.

Write Your Own Ending

Danny Meyer is an acclaimed restaurateur in New York and an active national leader in the fight against hunger. In his book *Setting the Table*, he discusses the transformative power of hospitality in restaurants, business, and life. Among the many useful concepts in this book, the idea of "writing a great last chapter" has helped me leverage many mistakes. According to Danny, when people encounter a problem during their restaurant experience, they are likely to tell more people about it than if everything went smoothly. So Danny found a way to use the mistakes that inevitably happen: *Turn them into an opportunity to deliver great service and promote the business.* When mistakes happen, he advises, the key is to move quickly to figure out how the rest of the story will be told. *How would his staff respond to their mistake?* Solving problems with generosity, learning, and grace actually builds loyal customers, rather than losing their business.

Solving problems with generosity, learning, and grace actually builds loyal customers, rather than losing their business.

We saw this in a young job applicant we interviewed. She was responsible for a situation with a caterer who delivered 300 gluten-free mini cupcakes a week ahead of a big party. Gluten-free cupcakes don't freeze well, so they couldn't save them. She explained that situation came about because the date was communicated in a phone call, and she had not confirmed it in writing, as she usually did, because it had been a particularly chaotic week. The caterer got the right day of the week, but the wrong week.

Taking on the problem and looking for a way to leverage it, she called various social service organizations who might be able to use the cupcakes, creating a lot of goodwill for themselves and the bakery. She worked with the caterer to redistribute the goodies. Next, she created a standardized checklist/template that would be used in all future orders to prevent that type of miscommunication from happening again. She and the caterer agreed to split the costs and continued to have a long and fruitful business relationship.

The pain of the miscommunication on her watch was mitigated by the results she was able to create. She didn't enjoy telling us about her mistake, but I could tell she was proud of the outcome and how facing such problems had changed her for the better. She saw it as unfortunate that it had occurred, but she was glad for the opportunity to learn something that would make her more successful in the future. As long as it happened, she might as well make the most of it.

Turning Mistakes into Stepping Stones

Learning and development alchemy happens when we transform our thinking, and therefore our response, to ultimately turn a mistake around. No matter how much planning and training experience you and your team have, *mistakes will happen.* When you take control of what happens after the mistake, you can turn those mistakes into gold. Of course, you will want to make it right, but you can do more than that—you can make moving forward *better.* Focusing your attention and the attention of those impacted on how well you and your team can respond changes the game from a blamefest to an opportunity to create a generous, sincere, and gracious ending.

Coming to terms with our shortcomings puts us one step closer to turning a situation around. Once you acknowledge that a mistake has occurred, you can use this simple protocol to address it:

The Mistake Protocol

1. Apologize to the person/people involved and acknowledge the problem.

2. Rectify the situation by mitigating it as best you can. (You may need to ask others for help and support.)

3. Prevent similar mistakes from happening in the future by looking for the cause or a systemic way to reduce the likelihood of it happening again.

4. Communicate your action plan to those involved in steps 1–3.

5. Write a great last chapter. Can this mistake, combined with a little creativity, be turned into a positive memory for you and others? Make a lasting positive change based on your graceful recovery.

Handling mistakes well can result in deep learning, recovery, and discovery. When mistakes become a catalyst for growth, we mitigate the damage by creating new capabilities, more confidence, and great stories to inspire others. Difficulties thus become the very bootstraps by which we can pull ourselves up to new levels.

WHY Do the Reflection Exercises?

» To recognize how past mistakes may actually have helped you grow.

» To reinforce your adoption of a deliberately developmental mindset.

» To reduce the fear of making mistakes.

» To increase your resilience and decrease your recovery time when things don't go well.

REFLECTION EXERCISES

Imagine yourself retired after a wonderful career. From that perspective, think of how you handled a recent big mistake or challenge.

1. How could this setback be a part of a larger arc of progress and success? What could be the best possible outcome?

2. Let's say you faced this situation more than once. How did you (would you) have handled it better the next time?

3. What happens when others make mistakes in your work or home life that impact you? What tools do you use to create learning or help the people impacted make the situation better?

4. Consider the last significant mistake you made.
    a. What did you do upon realizing it?
    b. How did you manage your emotions in the midst of it?
    c. Is this how you usually respond to mistakes you make?
    d. What changes, if any, would help you better leverage mistakes for learning next time?

5. How will you apply what you have learned from recent mistakes as you go forward?

The most difficult thing is the decision to act; the rest is merely tenacity. The fears are paper tigers. You can do anything you decide to do. You can act to change and control your life; and the procedure, the process is its own reward.

—AMELIA EARHART
first female aviator to fly solo across the Atlantic Ocean

PART THREE

SELF-DIRECTED GROWTH THE WILLINGNESS SHIFTS

INCREASING *willingness* clarifies and focuses us; it helps us discern what is ours to do—and what *isn't*. Sometimes it hurts to see where we need to grow, but that doesn't stop us. When you decide to affirmatively go after the things that matter and let the less important tasks drop away, you have prepared for change and alignment with your personal mission.

THE SHIFT:

—FROM—

"My development goals
are a low priority"

—TOWARD—

"Investing in myself grows
my value and contribution."

12

OWN YOUR LEARNING

If you're not making use of even the most routine
assignment to learn something, realize that many
of your colleagues and co-workers are.

—ADENA FRIEDMAN
President and CEO of NASDAQ

SOPHIE WAS ON A TEAM of database specialists. Her work was quite good; she was always ready to dig in and deliver. I enjoyed working with her. At the time, I was in one of my first roles as a manager, and I attempted to support her with project information, counsel, and professional development suggestions. She was a solid player—consistent, upbeat, and a good communicator, but she wasn't seen by others as having high potential. And she wasn't growing.

After working together for a couple years, I confronted Sophie about her lack of improvement in the depth and breadth of her expertise and abilities. There was nothing wrong with her work quality or productivity, but she wasn't growing enough to advance, and that bothered me. The opportunities to develop were there, but she never made time for them. She always gave perfectly reasonable explanations for why she could not redirect her focus, such as "Maybe after this big database is rebuilt," or "I need to be on hand to support Evan as he gets up to speed for the next couple months." However, when a pattern of short-term "explanations" goes on for years, the reasons sound more and more like excuses. She probably felt she was doing what the company needed of her, but only from a very limited perspective. I doubt she realized she was sacrificing her advancement and her long-term goals.

Investing in oneself, even when there is no problem with the current work quality, teamwork, or capability, may seem counterintuitive when there are so many other demands. However, in our fast-paced, ever-changing world, if you are not advancing your learning, you are steadily falling behind.

Even if you are not inherently competitive or concerned about "keeping up" with others, the many dimensions of work opportunities to develop our skills—technical, social, creative, systemic, collaborative, etc.—can advance capabilities or leave us in the dust of those advancing past us. The difference is primarily in how we choose to respond to the opportunities for learning that present themselves to us every day. I'm sure you've seen people become less valuable and relevant as your industry evolves—and you've seen others grow their value, marketability, and prowess in response to the constant changes around them.

Which group do you want to be part of?

Staying Relevant

In technology, the need for growing our skills could not be clearer. It's not uncommon for an excellent programmer, once sought after by leading-edge product development teams, to be relegated to maintaining or integrating legacy systems if she doesn't learn new programing languages or master new platforms. The world seems to change with each new wave of young programmers who force the next disruption in the industry. When people resist learning new approaches, they have a lot of reasonable-sounding excuses. Unfortunately, the more they give in to those excuses, the more they outdate themselves. On the other hand, building new capabilities in addition to what you already can do broadens your base of understanding and your ability to address complex problems. This allows you to contribute in new and more substantial ways.

Learning ourselves forward thus becomes a discovery process, an experiment of finding what works, what matters, what doesn't—and how to improve what we do and clarify what we stand for.

But this is not the only reason to venture outside your comfort zone to explore the outer edges of your playing field and develop new capabilities. Things such as teamwork, interpersonal communication, project management, personal productivity, and presentation skills are assets you can use throughout life. They are your personal portable capital. Why wouldn't you want to use your current work experience as the foundation—or even launching pad—to your next one?

The second reason for investment in oneself is that it enhances your engagement. Investing in your growth heightens your commitment to understanding, knowledge, and insight. Curious engagement, when applied to our self-development and careers, has tremendous impact in our overall lives. We prime our readiness for whatever our future holds by being willing to take a baby step—then another, then another—closer each time to who we want to become. *Learning ourselves forward thus becomes a discovery process, an experiment of finding what works, what matters, what doesn't—and how to improve what we do and clarify what we stand for.*

As students, many of us were trained to wait until our teacher showed us what we should be learning. Unless we were very lucky, it was usually out of step with our interests. It was hard to engage with beyond what it took to get a decent grade. Becoming a *self-directed* learner, ready to influence the causes we care about, drives our agenda for self-initiated development. It becomes the impetus to take on the challenges we might otherwise shy away from.

The Third Paycheck is ours to use wherever we want. It doesn't matter if no one asks us to develop these new skills and capacities. In just about any role, you can intentionally seek out and design your own developmental assignments. Practical, on-the-job development combines getting a job done with growing oneself at the same time.

Test Your Willingness

Imagine you've decided to step into an expanded role on a work project to further your own learning. Which of the following would help you develop a higher level of engagement and leadership?

» Speaking up during a meeting to be more influential and effective at conveying information others need to understand.

» Asking clarifying questions to determine the criteria that will be used to assess if the project is being done well.

» Using your reflection time to ask, "What if . . ." and imagine what would happen if this project were wildly successful. What are the positive potential futures? What one action could you take to help make the best of those futures more likely?

» Think through the linkages between current tasks and the overall strategic direction of the organization. How does this project relate to the whole? How do your actions tie into upper management's strategic objectives? (If you're unsure of what they are, ask.)

» Do you see any holes in the current plan? Write what you know about the situation and how you propose to address it before you bring it up. Update your understanding and your approach as you learn more information along the way.

» Volunteer to lead a specific task within the project and then ask for feedback about your leadership.

» Collaborate with colleagues to redesign a process that isn't working well.

» Take on a responsibility that is currently "falling through the cracks" or not being given proper priority.

» Make a point of appreciating the contributions of a team member—encourage and support them, in person and with a note or email.

» Reach out to another department or peer to discuss a project cross-functionally. Document their points of view for future reference.

As you read each of these "assignments," notice your initial reaction and how willing you would be to take one or more of them on as growth steps. Which feel like they would be a good fit for something you want to learn? Or are there better options than the examples above—options that would be more interesting or hold more potential for growth?

If none of these seems feasible or piques your interest, perhaps you should look inside instead. Do you feel resistant to investing in yourself in one of these ways? Is there some other personal "pain point"—a sense of impatience, a short fuse, shyness, uncertainty, a knowledge deficit, a skill you've never mastered, etc.—that you feel you should work on instead? What causes you to fear or question your ability to contribute? What other area or skill would it be better for you to work on first?

The point is to find some area where you want to grow and give yourself permission to engage with some fresh learning, new ideas, and different perspectives so you can keep your developmental juices flowing.

Once you've chosen something specific, what would your own customized "program" to address that item look like? What developmental assignments, readings, journaling, volunteering, relationship building, or coursework would you prescribe for yourself to get more mastery in that area? Or maybe there's someone you should take out for coffee or a lunch?

Perhaps it's not a work item at all that you want to get better at or know more about. Consider taking a course in a totally different field than your current work to see what insights arise. The point is to find some area where you want to grow and give yourself permission to engage with some fresh learning, new ideas, and different perspectives so you can keep your developmental juices flowing. Learning how to learn—how to master a new field or get better at something—is a skill worth sharpening.

Take Full Advantage of Professional Development

Investing in yourself means making the most of learning opportunities that come your way—whether you orchestrate them or they are required of you. When your workplace offers a day of "professional training," be sure you're ready to take full advantage of it.

Over the years, I've been to many types of learning sessions. Some were wonderful, others mediocre, and a few were painfully bad. However, no matter what information is provided by the presenter (useful or not), you can always create value for yourself worthy of the investment you made to attend. Before going to a training of any kind, consider the following tips:

> **Build Relationships.** Much of what we need to know to be successful is shared informally among those who have had experience with similar circumstances and are willing to share. When you attend a training, an important benefit can be the professional relationships you form with other attendees. Find people who have experience in what you are interested in. Talk to them, and, if possible, follow up with a meeting to discuss the topic further. If there is a panel or series of presenters, you may want to connect with one of them online after the event to provide feedback or ask them for more information. You may find people you can add to your network. Such contacts can be invaluable for learning about others' view of the issues that interest you or affect your industry.

> **Immediately Apply New Practices or Techniques.** Training without follow-up is useless. When there is a deeper understanding of the topic because you already

have a basic grasp of it, don't allow yourself to get bored. Instead, spend your time during and after the training figuring out how to better put the knowledge to use.

Share Information. Find a way to present your experiences, formally or informally. Not only does it give you practice with presentation skills, but when you organize information and convey it in a concise format, it also forces you to clarify your understanding. Teaching is a terrific way to learn more deeply. Exactly how will you convey what you know? Such preparation can be useful beyond the training day if you're willing to recycle it as a presentation to co-workers or other stakeholders who need the knowledge. Sometimes I practice sharing new leadership insights with my family. I know if I can keep their interest, I'm sure to be successful in the next training I lead. Use whatever opportunities are available to you to solicit feedback and refine your message.

Mentor Others. There's nothing like giving back. Younger co-workers or less knowledgeable peers will often appreciate your support, guidance, and assistance. Give it freely. You can offer support during the training itself, during breaks, or afterward back on the job. These acts honor those who have supported you in the past and pay it forward for others to support you in the future. (For more on the value of giving versus taking, see Adam Grant's book on that topic or his TED Talk.[15])

Shape your future by investing in yourself and learning your way forward. There's no better way to increase the value and impact of your Third Paycheck.

Do the Reflection Exercises?

- » To remove obstacles to investing in your development.

- » So you can stay relevant in your field.

- » To enable you to be more deliberately developmental.

- » So you will be more engaged and inspired by choosing to grow.

REFLECTION EXERCISES

1. List ten reasons investing in your development will benefit you, your organization, or those you care about.

2. Is there resistance or anxiety associated with investing in yourself? What do you see as the source of those feelings? What do you think would change this?

3. Think of someone you love. How have you encouraged them to invest in themselves and grow?

4. Who can reinforce your learning and encourage you to invest in yourself? How might you engage them or be inspired by them?

5. Look for inspiration in stories of learning and growth. Can you identify any examples of people who have invested in themselves to move forward in their career or for a cause? What lessons can you learn from their experiences?

6. If you were going to fully invest in yourself to move closer to fulfilling your personal mission, how would you plan your development? What could be a next (or first) step?

THE SHIFT:

—FROM—

"Making knee-jerk emotional responses"

—TOWARD—

"Letting intense emotion cue conscious choices."

NAVIGATING EMOTIONAL TRIGGERS

Humility in the face of the complex,
dynamic, uncertain world in which we all live
and work is simply realism.

—AMY EDMONDSON
Harvard Business School professor
and author of *Teaming*

BOB WAS IN HIS OFFICE, pinching the bridge of his nose, *hard*. He could not *believe* that he had inherited this group of managers. It was like herding teenagers. This was the year he had finally achieved a step up, a chance at senior leadership—and his reward was inheriting this group!

His span of control had grown considerably. He had long imagined the thrill of taking on higher-level challenges, making system-wide changes, and receiving increased visibility. As he considered the broader impact of his work, he was excited to be able to contribute at this level.

But this team!

What a disappointment. He had expected to be able to pull from a talented pool of professionals to make his vision a reality, but that was just not happening.

Bob replayed their last meeting in his mind. The team had complained ad nauseam without offering solutions. The next day, one manager had the audacity to request time off during their busiest week of the year, without a plan for coverage. Where was her ownership of the results? She just looked down at the desk when he confronted her on it and said it was the only time the rest of her family was free. When he tried to get people to open up about the underlying issues he sensed were there (but couldn't identify), they barely said anything. Individually each was nice enough, and several had the potential to make significant contributions to the field, but *together*? Together they were a chaotic mess.

Bob did not feel comfortable talking to his boss about these problems. He was afraid he would sound like a whiner. Instead, he went to a colleague. He shared some of the problems he'd seen. His colleague listened closely, and, to Bob's surprise, suggested that the problems could very well be coming from a team needing more direction and leadership.

What?

She explained, "Sometimes the most effective teams appear to have conflict. We should all be so lucky, really. It seems this way because they have enough cohesion, relationship credits, and strength to speak openly about what is not going well. They express their true feelings rather than holding back—and *that's a good thing.*"

She suggested he watch some videos about *Teaming* by Amy Edmondson.[16] "Lower-performing, less-effective teams don't say what they think," she went on, "so while there may be less visible discontent in meetings, they don't actually deal with important issues. People in teams without trust shut down and may be too scared to speak. Honestly talking about the issues at hand, even if they aren't doing it gracefully, is usually the foundation of a highly effective team."

Bob mulled this over. Maybe the problem wasn't the team members. Maybe he was just bristling at their conflict because it was different from what he had expected.

Their weekly meeting was scheduled for four hours to be sure all of the relevant issues could be addressed. He usually dove right in to the first agenda item once things were called to order. They needed to be efficient, after all. But the teaming materials had suggested he ask a warm-up question to bring the group together first. *Did they really need to "check in" with each other personally? Weren't they all professionals?* The suggestion sounded touchy-feely. Still, he could try it once. When it failed, he could be sure his first instinct was better.

However, when he tried it, he noticed that the feel of the rest of the meeting was distinctly better than usual. It was like a little of the edge had come off of their disagreements.

After the meeting, he found himself wondering if the people on his team understood why they were supposed to be working together. Then he wondered, *Are they supposed to be working together?* At least two of the team members didn't really have much interdependency with the rest, and maybe they didn't belong in most of the discussions. What was in their common interests? Was there a way to bring people together more? Was there a way for him to create more common ground?

Bob began to see his anger and insecurity had been triggering unhelpful responses. With that, he decided the best place to start would be with his own attitude. Feeling angry, disappointed, and frustrated certainly wasn't helping him listen, respond, or connect to his team members very well. He was far too impatient and dismissive. Slowing down to look at people and appreciate them as human beings was hard for his cut-to-the-chase, get-things-done style of leadership—*really hard*. Slowing down did help improve his listening, though, so the next meeting he decided to start asking more questions and giving fewer directives.

When he started getting curious about the team members' views and how they thought things could be more effective, the tide shifted—and quickly. They began to think out loud with him about the business issues and what each could do to address them. As Bob continued to dial down his emotional reactions to conflict and made more conscious choices about what he said and how he said it, their gains in productivity were surprising—exceeding his expectations time and again.

Steady in the Storm

Research shows that positive emotional and mental states increase self-awareness, empathy, communication, and resilience. This results in sustained peak performance, strong collaboration, effective leadership, and an inspiring personal presence. People who have "done their emotional work" tend to demonstrate a calm, unflappable self-mastery. They add tremendous value to an organization.

When we consider the significant impact of emotions on our work lives, it just makes sense to get smarter about them and learn how to have more mastery of our responses. The concept of "emotional intelligence" is attributed originally to researchers Dr. John D. Mayer of Stanford and Dr. Peter Salovey at Yale. They started discussing it in 1990. They conducted research on the impact of emotion on behavior and published several articles about its importance. The concept was then popularized and augmented by Daniel Goleman in his 1996 book *Emotional Intelligence: Why It Can Matter More Than IQ*.

Someone with high emotional intelligence can recognize, understand, and manage his or her emotions, as well as recognize, understand, and influence the emotions of others. Conscious choice, self-regulation, understanding motivations, exhibiting empathy, delaying gratification, and effective social skills are all traits that evolve along the continuum of increasing emotional intelligence.

Self-regulation is how you move from an emotion-ruled or lizard-brain-triggered automatic reaction to consciously selecting a response that will further goals and uphold values. Such self-control is a sign of a person's character, because the reason we choose to restrain our instinctual reaction demonstrates a commitment to honorable behavior, especially when the going gets tough. Reflexively, we all experience base emotions. They arrive unbidden. When someone provokes you and your anger makes you feel like lashing out and hitting them (they "push your buttons"), emotional intelligence helps you *choose* to respond differently. That's self-regulation. Although you are upset, you choose your behavioral response rather than letting emotion dictate your actions.

This level of awareness—and the ability to push the "pause" button between stimulus and reaction—is challenging to do, but it's a very human step to take. It is challenging because humans have an acute sense of danger and a corresponding chemical cascade that physiologically moves us into fight or flight, without allowing time for conscious thought. The amygdala, a little part of the limbic system on the underside of the brain, gets stimulated by potential threats and causes intense emotions such as aggression or fear. These reactions are far faster than our cognitive functions. That's why we react faster and more subliminally than conscious analysis permits.

So how can we behave as conscious professionals when our responses are hijacked by our biology before we are even aware of it? The civility of our workplaces and other communities depends on people increasing their awareness of their own emotional state and retaining choice about how to respond. For most of us, maintaining our integrity and consistently doing the right thing takes a lifetime of effort, marked by incremental improvements.

People at all levels in the working world are noticing that how they feel is a key component to their work satisfaction, engagement, and effectiveness.

Paradoxically, the best way to make progress is to stop trying to change anything and start observing yourself and your reactions to other people. "Why do I feel this way?" is an incredibly powerful and important question.

Making Your Emotions an Ally

Today, many companies are beginning to recognize the advantages of high emotional intelligence in hiring, relationship building, mentoring, teaming, conflict management, and change initiatives. People at all levels in the working world are noticing that how they feel is a key component to their work satisfaction, engagement, and effectiveness. Our feelings have many productive roles to play in our work. They are the basis for the Second Paycheck. Growing more aware and sensitive to the emotional tones in ourselves and others allows us greater access to our intuition and a whole suite of soft skills. Positive thoughts and emotions are at the forefront in leadership and organizational effectiveness research. They are consistently shown to invigorate and engage employees and leaders.[17]

Keeping your cool, especially under pressure, gives you more response options. Granted, your first, knee-jerk emotional response isn't always the best, so when something triggers you, notice what you would like to move *from* and *to*:

> When my office mate asks me a question, I will move *from* impatience and irritation *to* being curious and resourceful.

The idea is to identify what you currently are doing so you can "catch" the reaction, in order to immediately switch to a more skillful and useful response. Those choices are yours to make.

For example, let's imagine that Bob has a co-worker who undermines one of his attempts at building trust among team members. This "interference" activates Bob's anger response. He is ready to take the co-worker to task and unload his frustration. But just as he opens his mouth, he realizes he's been triggered. He slows his reaction. Instead of lashing out in anger, he notices he's angry, and then reacts *to* the anger, asking himself why it's been triggered. In the past, Bob would have not hesitated to forcefully communicate exactly what behavior was unacceptable and the consequences for further infractions. If his anger at the behavior showed through, so much the better, as he wanted the person to know not to repeat this performance. But this time he slowed down and remembered:

> When I feel anger rise at others' behavior I move *from* attacking them as an adversary *to* figuring out what

they were trying to accomplish.

Using this method, Bob was more frequently able to prevent his emotions from controlling his behavior, leading to more response options for him.

Instinctively, he started using the same method at home when his kids were bickering. (Sometimes, we import experiences in our home or community into the workplace to show us how to work productively with a diversity of opinions and types of people. Sometimes it's the other way around; the skills we learn on the job help us to lead a highly charged political conversation with a friend or manage a situation in our faith community.)

In our highly connected, instantaneously communicating world, successfully responding to emotional triggers has become increasingly important for those wanting to influence a broader playing field. If you are on a long-term mission, you'll need your emotions as an ally.

WHY Do the Reflection Exercises?

» To be able turn conflict with colleagues into learning.

» To increase your emotional intelligence and effectiveness in high stakes situations.

» So you can improve decision making and communication under pressure.

» To bring more awareness to your choices.

REFLECTION EXERCISES

1. Think back to a time within the past year when you were feeling
    a lot of emotion, something that upset you enough
    that it was hard to stop revisiting it over and over.

    a. How would you describe the primary emotion you
       were feeling?
    b. Why was that driver so strong at the time? Is it still strong?
    c. Where is it located in your body? What did it feel like?
    d. How did your mood or energy level affect your response?
    e. Ideally, how would you like to respond to this emotion in
       the future?

2. What shift can you make to reduce the impact of this trigger
    on you?

3. Are you aware of any early warning signs that you nearing
    strong emotional response? (Holding your breath, tension in
    chest or shoulders, locked jaw, the tone of your voice changes?)

4. Who might have some helpful ideas to support thinking through
    new response options?

5. Formulate your development intention:

    a. What do you call your main trigger?
    b. What response would you like to move away *from*?
    c. What response would you like to move *to*? (Select
       something that is challenging, but possible.)

6. Imagine yourself in a situation where you are triggered and
    see yourself choosing to respond in a new way. How could you
    improve your odds of having a consciously controlled response?

THE SHIFT:

—FROM—

"Doing what has
always been done"

—TOWARD—

"Focusing on what
matters most."

14

STRATEGIC PRIORITIES

Spend 80 percent of your time
on the three most important activities
that will bring you the greatest results.

—JENNIFER WHITE
author of *Work Less, Make More*

MANY OF THE LEADERS I work with are starting an organization, initiating a program, or taking over a department—or they're
repairing something that has become dysfunctional. The new
challenges or opportunities they are facing eclipse the skillsets
they built previously, and now they need new ways of thinking
and acting to be successful. The willingness to choose the path
of growth in the face of these difficulties is a key differentiating
factor between those who find workable solutions and those who
fall back into old, less-effective patterns.

If you are not willing to call into question your current set of
assumptions, you lock yourself inside the box of your old ones.
You're going to want to know how to question the utility of the
approaches that brought you to this point, so you can update them
in the light of what is changing around you and what is important

to you at this stage of your development. The ticket that lets you enter the realm of strategic priorities is openness to think about your leadership relative to what is happening *now* inside and outside your organization.

Ron experienced this firsthand. He had recently been promoted to the head of a healthcare association. He had skills from his previous work in hospitals—both as a clinical staff person and an administrator—but running an association for health organizations was a new world with different politics, priorities, and possibilities. To get his arms around it, he needed approaches not yet in his repertoire. He needed to grow into the position if he hoped to find satisfaction in his work.

The association was created because the hospitals and clinics wanted to coordinate to expand services where needed and eliminate overlap. Now there was plenty of care available, but there were still too many people falling between the cracks. There were duplications of certain specialties and lack of access to others. Looking at the original mission and objectives of the association, Ron realized they needed to start over.

He and I made a list together of the strategic objectives he needed to let guide him in the months to come:

1. **Clarify the association's mission**: What would be its primary strategy for the next few years?

2. **Determine his personal objectives in his new role**: What was at stake for him? What was going to make this job a fulfilling assignment over the next two to five years there?

3. **Foster alignment with other leaders**—board members and staff—on the purpose of the organization and its primary strategy for the coming two years.

4. **Develop a culture that aligned with the mission and strategy,** staffed with skilled, flexible, high-quality people willing to work together to grow the organization's impact and effectiveness.

5. **Reinforce the changes under way with system-wide training and development** for leaders throughout the facilities that were part of the association, as well as for the association employees.

Ron would work on these strategic priorities over the next two years. As he did, he also got clearer on his personal mission and value as a leader. He earned the appreciation and respect from the healthcare communities he served, and he became a voice in the industry trade groups. This extended his impact and helped him build a strong network of professional peer relationships across the country. The collective wisdom of the network he helped connect became an amazing resource for driving their mission forward.

Setting Strategic Priorities

We set strategic priorities by looking objectively outside ourselves and seeing what the situation calls for, prioritizing what matters most, and learning where we need to grow new capabilities. Strategic priorities are commitments you make because they address a critical success factor—something needed to complete the journey you are on. A strategic priority is bigger than a project. It's a series of projects and tasks that, once completed, add up to a significant whole. It's going to take some experimentation and reinvention to figure out the highest-leverage moves, what you can do easily, and what will take more time. Determining strategic priorities often pushes us into areas where we don't know what we don't know. Part of the journey is growing ourselves enough to be able to see the next steps.

As we follow Ron's strategic trajectory, take note of the interplay between growing himself and designing the organization as a platform for creating positive impact.

1. Clarifying the Association's Mission

When the mission of an organization isn't clear, it's hard to know what your strategic priority is. To get clarity, Ron reviewed the existing strategic plans and began talking with members and staff one-on-one to find out what resonated with what they felt was needed. He wanted to focus on the highest calling of the organization first. What was it capable of accomplishing? What was it uniquely able to do, which no one else could do as well? Then he added his own thoughts into the mix: *What mission would I be proud to lead?*

Ron had been an EMT early in his career, and one of his patients died because the care facility Ron worked for was understaffed. He was put in a position where he could not attend to two patients adequately at the same time, a heartbreaking, impossible situation that cost a life. It became a defining moment in Ron's career.

As a result, Ron understood the power of trade-offs. He had an intense desire to keep people out of impossible situations like the one he'd experienced. He listened deeply to really understand what was important to the people who worked for him. Then he partnered with them to build solutions that made sense to all involved.

In the process, Ron became aware of a personal growth edge: He got frustrated easily when they weren't making progress. He found it hard to balance that impatience for action and his need to listen deeply to others. He began disciplining himself to slow down, and he initiated discussions with his team on how they could be mindful of the pace of their interactions, taking the time to understand their perspectives, and then create space to design and test solutions to find out what would work best before moving forward.

Using a similar method with his board, he gathered input and worked collaboratively to align around the common needs of the members, enabling them to clearly identify the mission that was shared and endorsed by all involved.

2. Determining His Own Buy-in

Clarifying the personal reasons for his role and his motivation wasn't hard for Ron. The experiences he'd had in healthcare and his desire to make care accessible and safe were front and center. What was at stake for him was where to most effectively invest his energy. Seeing high-quality healthcare accessible to anyone who needed it was a personal goal. It really mattered to him to make progress in that particular area, and life is short.

He took on the job because of this personal mission, and he wanted to make significant gain toward accomplishing it during his tenure. He intended to spend time leading toward something that would have a profound impact on the lives of those seeking treatment at their facilities. He was willing to learn whatever was needed to make progress.

This clarity of purpose combined with his willingness and motivation was a huge leverage point for resilience and grit when the work became taxing, confusing, and complicated. His deliberate developmental focus set the conditions for success in motion.

3. Fostering Alignment with Other Leaders

Alignment is the calibration among different perspectives and objectives around common ground that everyone agrees makes sense, even if it's not a perfect solution for all involved. It can be "on the way" even if it isn't "all the way." If you can get 80 percent of your desired outcome, along with the endorsement of others by getting their objectives met, that's better than the alternatives. Creating such alignment holds communities and associations together. Holding out for a perfect match, thus stalling progress on the whole thing or starting over somewhere else, makes progress much slower.

Creating alignment requires a specific type of leader who can be factual, persuasive, and accommodating.

Creating alignment requires a specific type of leader who can be factual, persuasive, and accommodating. It involves a flexibility and a persistence to build a shared understanding of what's going on, to see what it means from different angles in the system, to have a little humor in the face of challenges, and to create a solid set of options for all to consider.

Ron had done some alignment work in small ways in other roles. He was glad he had some of the basics down, because now in the CEO chair, the stakes were higher, and most of the players were senior executives themselves. And everyone was watching.

He was proud of the team he assembled: staff, consultants, allies on the board, and partner organizations who helped him brainstorm about building a unified coalition and then stayed with him to help accomplish their shared mission over the next eighteen months. The prior CEO had failed to accomplish the same level of alignment in more than six years at the helm. Ron felt deep satisfaction in what they'd been able to achieve.

4. A Culture Aligned with Mission and Strategy

To develop a culture that aligned with its mission and strategy, Ron addressed some specific, recent examples that didn't feel like a culture that supported the strategy or had the right skill level to do the work that needed to be done. He confronted these situations one by one, cleaning them up and adjusting the systems around them to be cohesive with the people they served.

One of his most innovative approaches was how he handled his project officer.

This project officer oversaw compliance with the terms of grants and the accomplishments of the programs they funded. The project officer Ron had for a major grant was brand-new, fresh out of college. She had little knowledge of what to do about important issues. Ron was frustrated and irritated that she was so ill-equipped, but he also knew she had a lot of power over him and his organization. He decided to build a culture of communication in this key relationship.

He contacted this project officer and made a suggestion: "How about sharing knowledge?" He proposed that since he was new in his role and she was new in hers, they could pool what they knew and learn faster. They could talk more frequently and discuss issues more broadly so they could both learn more about the context and the issues for the grant. She agreed.

It was a slow process of building a collegial relationship, and there were big gaps in the project officer's knowledge of her role. However, Ron's method of working on it was so proactive, kind, and useful that she really appreciated it. His method stood out in contrast to the choices made by other grantees she worked with. Ron built a key, mutually supportive relationship with the project officer by getting past his personal judgment about what someone should already know before being assigned a role. He took a long-term approach with many short-term benefits. His calls with her had more laughter now, and they were more effective, although it cost him almost twice as much time as he originally intended to spend managing this grant. In the end, he felt the investment paid off.

Months later, Ron transitioned the relationship again. He really wanted the project officer to understand their successes as well as their challenges and issues, so he set a calendar appointment on the twentieth of each month to remind himself to send a quick email to her with a news clipping, success story, or win for the month. "Just keeping you in the loop!" he'd say. It let him stay in touch as well as share good things that were happening because of their grant.

Building a set of strategic priorities in any role involves similar steps to those Ron took, starting with an objective view of what is going on—awareness—with a clarity about which approach you are willing to commit to and others can support. After all, it should help them achieve their objectives too. Strategic priorities combine the view from the balcony and intersecting objectives with your own clarity of purpose to pinpoint the activities that will truly make a difference to you and your organization's mission.

WHY Do the Reflection Exercises?

» To define your strategic priorities and gain clarity on your mission as a leader.

» So you can make sure you are investing your time, energy, and focus in the right areas.

» To work smarter, focusing on what matters.

» In order to strategically plan toward goals that will bring you fulfillment and meaning.

REFLECTION EXERCISES

1. Looking broadly at your career history until now, pause and consider your strategic priorities. What have you focused on?

2. Imagine yourself moving forward in time to where you intend or hope to head next in your career. What is most important about that future?

3. What do you want to accomplish? What would achieving it make possible?

4. What needs to be in place to allow it to happen?

5. What skills or abilities would increase the likelihood of success? Where can you build alignment, support, or partnership with others to gain these skills and accomplish your priorities?

6. What next steps will help you focus on what matters most?

THE SHIFT:

—FROM—

"Giving in or running
from fear and self-doubt"

—TOWARD—

"Investigating fear and doubt
to glean what can be learned."

15

THE MESSAGE OF
FEAR AND DOUBT

Remember that no one is born a change maker.
It's something you become when you see a
problem, then dare to become part of the solution.

—MELINDA GATES
Co-founder of the Bill & Melinda Gates Foundation

AS A YOUNG GIRL, Louise watched the play-it-safe kids on ice skates. They would twirl and glide beautifully, flawlessly, but she never saw them try what they didn't already know how to do. Louise liked to learn new tricks, so she experimented and fell—a lot—usually ending up sliding across the ice on her rear end. While having a snowy butt wasn't glamorous, it was the way she learned new moves, and she loved the learning—even if not so much the falling down in front of others. Sometimes Louise envied those who were more graceful and poised, but she wasn't about to let feeling self-conscious stop her, especially when the others stood watching as she finally succeeded in landing a jump or coming out of a spin. She wasn't about to trade in that feeling for anything, even if it meant she had cold, wet pants on the way home.

Now a professional in her thirties, Louise smiled about those days, appreciating that she was still willing to try new stuff, even if it meant she might get a "snowy butt." She learned not to focus on the fear when she wasn't sure of what she was doing or when she heard that *Who do you think you are?* voice in her head. Instead, she motivated herself by focusing on doing her part, supporting her team, and finding the best solutions, even if that sometimes meant taking risks. Sure, sometimes she knew she was stepping out on a limb and felt the risk shake her to the core, but that was beside the point. Those feelings were just something she had to deal with along the way, like traffic and difficult people. So she learned to handle the uncertainties about how a meeting might go—or what her boss might say if she presented him with her honest opinion—with the same grace she used to get up off the ice and brush the snow from her backside.

Working through Fear

Getting to the other side of fear feels good. Liberating. Accomplished. It builds trust in ourselves and our abilities, helping us stretch further out to our next scary edge and then conquer that too. Accepting fear as natural feedback that we are trying something outside of our comfort zone, and then dealing with it as such, helps us realize our potential. Sometimes fear warns us of something to avoid, or that we need to proceed with increased caution. Overcoming fear and anxiety doesn't mean we won't feel them the next time we stretch, but we can face them more confidently, and, hopefully, handle them a little better each time.

Every successful and accomplished senior professional has faced doubt, fear, and worry. *Every single one.* These are not signs of weakness. These emotions are signs of pushing boundaries;

they are signs of creating opportunity. They are a call for you to investigate the feelings to find out more. Chances are, your fear is evidence that you are on the path to new growth—or what Steven Pressfield characterizes as "Overcoming Resistance," the thing that gets between us and our best selves:

> Every sun casts a shadow, and genius's shadow is Resistance. As powerful as our soul's call to realization, so potent are the forces of Resistance arrayed against us. . . .
>
> Resistance is experienced as fear; the degree of fear equates to the strength of Resistance. Therefore the more fear we feel about a specific enterprise, the more certain we can be that that enterprise is important to us and to the growth of our soul. That's why we feel so much Resistance. If it means nothing to us, there'd be no Resistance.[18]

Leaders are constantly presented with challenges that require them to rise up to another level. These challenges stretch us and ask us to test ourselves—to move to the developmental edge and try something new. In the process, we show ourselves and others that we can accomplish a difficult, or even seemingly impossible, feat.

This is exactly how we grow and develop on the job, in our volunteer work, in our community, and in family relationships. Being willing to take on a challenge when the outcome isn't certain is part of the path to growth.

Inspiring bosses and supervisors are usually learning and growing themselves, facing their own fears, and modeling what it looks like to balance risk with forward progress.

And this is also how we lead authentically. Inspiring bosses and supervisors are usually learning and growing themselves, facing their own fears, and modeling what it looks like to balance risk with forward progress. We demonstrate our leadership when it's time to rise to the next level of our ability and have the courage to find a way forward, even when the outcome is uncertain.

Getting Unstuck

When we face our fears, we can examine them and find out how relevant they are. Sometimes, we find they don't relate to our current situation. They are born of ordeals from our past, or gremlins in our psyche. These fears are noise in the system, echoes of old experiences or conversations that don't have much bearing on the current circumstances. We're just having a reflex reaction to stimuli we've experienced before and it overpowers us. When we recognize this, we can choose to respond more consciously.

You can reduce the risk to create a less-stressful path moving forward, or you can "face your fears and do it anyway." That's how courage works.

The objective is not to get rid of fear, to be ashamed of it, or to make it stop. It is to feel it, learn from it, move forward, and not let it prevent us from growing. We do not need to do everything that scares us to be successful, thank goodness, but fear may show us where to stretch, or how to break free from old patterns and find better ways to accomplish the results we seek. We learn to live with fear, to listen to it, and to make shifts so we can succeed anyway. Traffic congestion doesn't go away, but it need not stop us from getting to our destination.

Facing our fears may also reveal potential risks, dangers, and hurdles where our chosen path might lead. Asking oneself, "Exactly *why* am I hesitant to move forward?" may show you important issues that need to be addressed to protect yourself. In this way, fear can be very instructive and offer guidance on becoming the type of human being you want to become, while avoiding unnecessarily dangerous pathways.

Asking yourself some of the following questions can help you weigh your options and determine the level of risk you are actually taking. When we look at the situation through these lenses, not only do we ease our fears, but we create greater motivation for moving forward.

1. What's the Worst that Could Happen?

It helps to look at the worst-case scenario in order to understand the actual risk you may encounter. Fears are sometimes founded in real threats, and at other times they are merely dark imaginings. To sort out which you are facing, you may want to quantify your assessment: *How bad is it really? How likely is it to happen?* Use percentages or a scale of 1–10. It helps create perspective from which your decisions can flow.

After you examine the worst-case scenario, compare the level of risk to your level of fear. Does it match? This helps you know where to focus. You can reduce the risk to create a less-stressful path moving forward, or you can "face your fears and do it anyway." That's how courage works.

2. What Could Go Right?

Next, give some time to the bright side. People frequently talk about a devil's advocate viewpoint, one that identifies what could go wrong or looks for all of the flaws in an idea. We give lots of airtime to that perspective when we talk about worst-case scenarios, but what about the other side? *What could go right? What advantages and possibilities could come from following this line of action?*

I like to call this the "angel's advocate" point of view: all the surprisingly beneficial results that could come from making whatever scary move we are considering.

Equal airtime is the standard we seek so that we spend as much time fantasizing about the potential, the opportunity—the *upside*—as we do about the dangers, risks, and possible *downside.* Mentally, identifying the benefits of a potential action creates more willingness, inspiration, and new options to help us find a way to move forward.

3. What Do You Stand *For*?

People often get very excited about what they're against, but an equally important—if not more important—question is *What are you for?* What do you believe in? What do you want to see more of in the world?

Have you experienced the difference between a manager who uses fear as a "motivation tool" and one who uses enthusiasm and human connection? It makes a world of difference in the workplace. Naturally, it also makes a world of difference in our own heads. Identifying *what you are for* motivates more willingness than focusing on what you are against. *What you are for*—a purpose, commitment, or vision—will help you do what you need to do, regardless of fear, doubt, and insecurity, because the difference you could make matters. Before we have the confidence to trust in ourselves, we can trust in a mission that calls for our best. We can trust that when we put our effort forward to achieve that intention, we are making a difference, however imperfectly. I have seen amazing professionals beat themselves up with fear—whipping themselves with anxiety-provoking thoughts and choices made to avoid a danger—rather than moving toward their highest calling. When we learn how to trust in our value, we can ease up on trying to motivate ourselves by either the use of fear or the avoidance of it.

4. Where Can I Receive Support?

Being a part of a group working on a project or having a friend or colleague go with you to an event can make it much easier to move forward in spite of feeling fear or anxiety. Living with our fear and moving forward to choose growth experiences can be fun, especially when we are sharing the adventure. The chemical release in the body that happens when we experience fear is virtually the same as when we experience excitement. If you like riding roller coasters, perhaps you know what I mean. (And I don't know anyone who thinks much about avoiding the experience of excitement.)

Having friends or colleagues on the journey with us can connect us to people who "get us" or who belong to peer communities where others are dealing with similar challenges. When humans face tough stuff, being connected and accountable to one another can mean the difference between moving past our fear or letting it undermine us.

5. What's the Next Simple Step?

When you are driving on a long journey, you can see only what is right in front of you through the windshield. Even though the journey may be across states or across the country, you have to focus your effort on going the next twelve feet, and then the next mile. You don't know what is around the bend. You can only position yourself to be ready to make good decisions when the next curve comes into view.

Successful people take risks by being brave for themselves and advocating for their dreams, but it's the same as driving across the country. At times you'll get off track, the GPS will develop a mind of its own, or you'll read your map wrong. Sometimes you'll even find something more interesting along the way and want to stay there longer. Dividing the trip into manageable segments makes room for adjustment along the way. Making room for decisions as you go might even help you see a better route or a preferable destination. Even when you don't know how it will work out, the experiments you run provide learning and get you farther down the road toward your final destination. That is success.

Cut through Fear with Meaning

We have limited time and energy, and it's important to say "no" to endeavors, people, and behaviors that will push us off track. When you clarify the contribution you want to make—in the moment or over a lifetime—you are staking out what matters to you. The connection to something greater than ourselves prompts us to find a way or pave a path to take action and move forward, despite the fear and doubt we may feel. Our personal mission calls forth our best. *We do what is required of us on our quest to make a difference, even when it is way outside our comfort zone.*

The rewards for this risk-taking are the life on the other side of fear and doubt, including the adventures we aspire to and the purposes we want to contribute to. When we face our fears and do what we need to do, learning and improving along the way, we step into leadership roles we never dreamt possible.

Do the Reflection Exercises?

» To give you room to investigate the value fear can bring to you.

» To change your relationship to fear and doubt.

» So you can practice using meaning, mission, and purpose to cut through fear.

» To enable you to see past your initial reaction and choose a more conscious response.

REFLECTION EXERCISES

1. Think of a specific developmental stretch that brings up fear or doubt. What does fear sound like in your head?

2. What does your fear value? What value do you hold that gives rise to these concerns? (Such as wanting to do high-quality work, or not wanting to hurt someone's feelings.)

3. Quantify the level of this fear or anxiety using the scale of 1-10 we talked about earlier.

4. What would make this situation more intense or scarier? What's the worst that could happen?

5. What would make this situation less scary or maybe even more exciting to attempt? What could go right? (Practice invoking the "angel's advocate" perspective.)

6. What mission or purpose would make it worthwhile to push past this fear into action?

THE SHIFT:

—FROM—

"Striving to 'find
my purpose'"

—TOWARD—

"Allowing what brings
me joy to lead me forward."

16

BREAD CRUMBS OF JOY

The pivot toward purpose-driven companies
comes from reflecting on my career journey.
I've been happiest and performed best when
my work was connected to a greater purpose that
galvanized people around a shared mission.

—MATT SONEFELDT
Head of Corporate Development at Gusto

IN 2012, I WAS HONORED to be a leadership coach at the Hesselbein Global Student Leadership Summit hosted by the University of Pittsburgh. Fifty college students prepared action plans to discuss their aspirations for how they wanted to change some part of the world they lived in. Many students had already done some work in their area of interest. Others were clarifying their intentions for the future when they graduated. Unanimously, the students were eager to learn strategies to help them move forward and make an impact.

I noticed some common themes among the conversations inspired by Frances Hesselbein's approach to being of service.

Among these student leaders there was a clear desire to help others, and, for many of them, their desires were based on life experiences. For instance, "Why are you interested in helping at-risk youth?" "Because I was one." Or "Why do you want to help girls develop their leadership potential?" "Because that's what made the biggest difference for me." This is one way to begin the path of purpose. Notice what mattered to you as a younger person—what did, and did not, support you—and look for opportunities to help others in the same way. Purpose is built from your experiences and intentions.

These students had a lot of big dreams, and it was often tough to counsel them on where to start. I find myself recommending those I advise to "try out" their ideas and interests by connecting with what is right in front of them—speaking on topics that interest them wherever they can, starting a pilot program, or building a small-scale version of a big idea to develop data, credibility, and evidence that their ideas work.

Mike was a student I met at the summit. He was living on a houseboat in Florida while attending college. We talked about the questions he was asking himself related to his action plan, and how to direct his attention to discover more about where his purpose might lead. He described his interests in both sailing and helping troubled high school kids get back on track, and how he was combining those into a program. He began by developing a theory of change: How could sailing help at-risk teens?

The next year, in 2013, Mike founded SailFuture as an after-school mentoring program in partnership with his college and a local high school. Learning to sail helped the kids develop trust, respect, and friendship with their college-aged mentors. This improved their chances of graduating from high school. He grew the project from there. Using the successes from his first small-scale program as proof of concept, he found new partnerships for the program, clarified its funding models, and built a robust and innovative organization.

Mike's purpose of making a difference for youth trapped in the juvenile justice system is having an impact, and it continues to grow. Today SailFuture* combines long-term housing, challenging sailing experiences, an accredited high school, life coaching, and job training to transform the lives of some of the most challenging youth in Florida's child welfare system.

Feeling a lack of purpose can create confusion and disillusionment. Many think they have to find their purpose before they throw themselves into working toward it. Others throw themselves into their job, get better at certain aspects of it, and then discover they have passions in areas that don't relate to their role. I'm sure you've heard the career advice, "Do what you love," but building a bridge from the work you currently do to what would be fulfilling for you can seem almost impossible. Don't give up hope. Look for the bread crumbs of joy.

Follow the Bread Crumbs

What are the little events that really make your day? What gives you little flashes of joy in the midst of your daily tasks? Where is the spark for you? What are you most excited to share or see in your work world? I consider such things to be bread crumbs along the path leading toward fulfillment and purpose. Each time we recognize one and follow it, we find ourselves a little closer to what connects us with meaning.

---

* Visit http://www.sailfuture.org for more information. "SailFuture's programs leverage challenging sailing experiences, counseling, experiential education, and long-term housing to help some of society's most challenging boys develop into independent young men." (From the website.)

I've seen this be effective for many clients. Each of us has an inner compass that points in the direction of our best use. It seems to be guided by our feelings—the things we pay attention to that spark energy or delight within us—the little bread crumbs of joy. Following these tends to be much easier than answering the big "What is your purpose?" question. When we connect to the things about a job that ignite little sparks inside of us, we connect to a visceral ability to guide ourselves toward what is most fulfilling, and we end up shaping our purpose as we go, discovering how to integrate who we are and what matters to us with the people and projects that are right in front of us.

Conversely, sometimes our anger, pain, or disgust at a situation clarifies what matters to us and how best to put our talents into action. These feelings are bread crumbs of purpose as well—just in reverse. An intense emotion—exhilaration *or* upset—is a sign of your values. It may be a sign of something that matters to you being violated or diminished. *Don't discount the value of knowing what you can't stand. It helps reveal what you stand for.*

Don't discount the value of knowing what you can't stand. It helps reveal what you stand for.

Following such bread crumbs creates focus and a sense of personal direction. Being able to articulate what matters to you is extremely useful when mentors or other supporters want to help you. On the journey of working purposefully, start by exploring options, then experiment and keep moving forward on your growth. Absorb the feedback your little joy and pain experiments provide. Orient toward what matters most to you. This will make your work more personal and relevant, whether or not you ever feel satisfied that you know the answer to the elusive "Why am I here?" question. Start working with what calls to you and go from there. You don't have to figure it out all at once. In fact, you're better off doing it little by little.

One client I coached had a deep love of improvement. Her sparks of joy related to optimism, incremental growth, and continuous effort. Whatever she did, she kept trying to make things better around her. Her motto became "I'm *The Little Engine that Could.*" (It's good to have fun with this. You'd be surprised how valuable keeping your sense of humor can be when pondering your tendencies. No need to take yourself too seriously.)

Of course, there may be many iterations and changes as you discover new ways to put your talents, ideas, and values to work creating great new opportunities. At some point in the future, when you can see further and have gained more wisdom and skill, you'll likely see new ways to refine or shift your focus. Meanwhile, you can start working toward this current version of your purpose to keep moving forward. It might not be perfect, but it's probably moving you in the right direction. As the old saying goes, "You can't steer a parked car." As you and the environment you find yourself in evolve, the next direction or path will become apparent.

Purpose stokes our willingness to do what is necessary, to be motivated to learn what we need to, and to venture way outside of our comfort zone for a reason that matters. The hard, sometimes thankless work that drives being of service fosters a greater sense of contentment than pursing self-absorbed interests, especially when our efforts are understood and valued by a community. Making forward motion on a compelling goal and having an individual or a community of support is the best way we can grow and strengthen our passions and ability to live and work on purpose. Rosa Parks explained this beautifully: "I would like to be remembered as a person who wanted to be free . . . so other people would also be free." She also shared, "Each person must live their life as a model for others."

> *Find something you care about and throw yourself and your talents into it. Get started. If it's not your best way forward, you'll know soon enough.*

Purpose is not something you find outside of yourself, like looking for a lost puppy. It is what you do with what you find right in front of you. Purpose determines how we relate to others, how we respond to circumstances, and what matters to us. It emerges from putting our caring into action in a way that is meaningful and feels meaningful because it improves the world around us, even if just a little bit.

When we pursue purpose in our everyday lives, we tend to find fulfillment more quickly. You don't have to wait to "figure it out" or "focus on your one, true thing" before you engage. Instead, find something you care about and throw yourself and your talents into it. Get started. If it's not your best way forward, you'll know soon enough.

In *The Purpose Economy*, Aaron Hurst says it this way:

> People gain purpose when they grow personally, when they establish meaningful relationships, and when they are in service to something greater than themselves. . . .

> From the small and mundane daily choices we make to systemic and historic impact, we strive to contribute to the well-being of the world around us.[19]

In daily events, we demonstrate what matters to us by how we behave. Our values show through in how we treat others, how we approach issues, and whether or not we take responsibility for what we *can* do. Purpose stokes our willingness to do what is right and what is necessary.

Your purpose is a crystallization of what matters to you and in what direction you are headed to serve your values. So, while you may or may not know where the journey will take you, enjoy the unfolding. Even if the road is long and full of twists and turns, that's okay; the unexpected adventures are what make it interesting.

WHY Do the Reflection Exercises?

» So you can be inspired by your "bread crumbs" of joy.

» So you'll stop trying to "figure it all out" before getting started.

» To reduce confusion and create a productive forward focus.

» To be of service to something greater than yourself.

REFLECTION EXERCISES

1. What experiences have you found deeply fulfilling? Make a list of eight to ten.

    a. What really mattered to you about those experiences? Why were they important to you?
    b. Look at these experiences from someone else's point of view: What would you conclude is really important to the person (you) who had them?
    c. What did you stand for when you experienced these things?

2. What kind of person are you?

    a. What type of things do you really care about?
    b. Why are those types of things important to you?
    c. What inspired you to care about those things?

3. How does what you care about influence the way you work? What motto or saying captures what really matters to you?

    a. Could this be a "hypothesis of a purpose" that you could test in some small way?

4. What capabilities will you need to move in the direction of your hypothesis, to experiment with it or test it?

5. Where in your current workplace can you start taking action in alignment with what you care about the most?

6   How can you take steps forward to build skills (start small), or learn what you need, even if you have uncertainties?

THE SHIFT:

—FROM—

"Whatever I can do,
I should"

—TOWARD—

"Being clear on what is,
and is not, mine to do."

DECIDING WHAT *NOT* TO DO

Competence is an intrinsic motivator.
It feels good to do things we do well.
It helps us show people we have talent, too.
The problem is, you're not helping yourself
or your team if you fail to let go of old tasks
and focus on helping others grow.

—JILL GEISLER
author of *Work Happy: What Great Bosses Know*

FROM HER HOSPITAL BED, Kendra texted the security protocols to ensure the client's go-live date wasn't missed. She had to be admitted because of a medical emergency, but as the senior member of the team, she was the only one who knew the essential information. Her expert knowledge was a source of strength and authority, but also a trap. Because she was devoted, competent, and precise in her technical prowess, her company didn't want to move her into leadership roles where she would be working at the higher-level system design. The trap of her expert focus was preventing her from securing a promotion to a higher-level leadership role.

Since she was spending all her time doing the technical aspects of her current job, and learning all about this client's requirements and protocols, she had no time to invest in building the skills of other team members who could be taking on this work or building relationships within the firm. When an opportunity came along to join another firm, she opted to leave her company; it was the only way she could see to get out of the trap.

You can choose *not* to invest in learning where it doesn't serve you. Even when the company asks. You can choose *not* to initiate something new or *not* take on a new role, even though you could probably figure it out. Even if you are a seasoned pro at getting a particular thing done, it doesn't mean you have to continue to grow your expertise in that specific area. Why would you choose to avoid learning or stop doing something you are already pretty good at? Personally and professionally, I've noticed "not doing" and "not learning" are methods employed by those who have chosen to focus on doing what matters most.[20] Being a conscious professional means paying attention to what matters *now*, and expecting that what matters will change and evolve over time, as you do.

Instead of trying to know-it-all, do-it-all, or learn-it-all, there are some areas you may choose to ignore for the sake of excelling somewhere more significant. Not doing those aspects of the work preserves your focus for priorities that are more important to you, your career, and your purpose. An added bonus is that stepping back gracefully, and supportively, makes room for others to shine at what would only be a distraction for you.

Though it's a counterexample, I've noticed that teens are unconsciously good at being strategically incompetent. If a teenage boy does a poor job of cleaning the kitchen, how likely is it that he will be asked to do it again? The effort of having to clean up after he "cleans up," wipe the counters he *didn't* wipe, and communicate the finer points of scrubbing, stove maintenance, and dishwasher loading while he rolls his eyes is pretty unpleasant for all involved. Given those trade-offs, "I'll just do it myself" can look pretty good. Or you may decide to hold him accountable for the results, regardless of the effort it takes, and help him understand your standards for a "clean kitchen," but that comes at a cost.

You are probably already seeing some parallels to the workplace. People use strategic incompetence in useful—or, like this teenager, not so useful—ways. It depends on their motivations. A serial entrepreneur with programming roots wanted to assure himself and his team that he would not be spending late nights redoing the programming of his staff. He needed to focus on building the company. Knowing how much he still loved to get his hands on the code, what could he do to resist the temptation? His answer was to arrange to have the next project his company built done in a programming language he didn't know. The new language was better, plus it curbed his ability to meddle. He couldn't even if he tried. These choices demonstrated skillful use of "strategic incompetence."

Similarly, an executive I know (with three kids) told me she doesn't know how to cook dinner, at least not anything other than heating something up. So rather than cook every night, they order out, or her stay-at-home husband cooks, or she buys things her kids can make. When she confided this to me, I looked at this capable project manager, accomplished baker, and incredibly smart woman, and I laughed out loud. Of course she could cook, *if she wanted to*. This wasn't a disability, but a very strategic choice not to know something—and I applauded it. When I asked her more pointedly about it, she agreed that, in theory, she certainly could learn how to cook great dinners. She just had no desire to do so, and it wouldn't help their family dynamics if she did.

Holding on Instead of Transitioning

In the workplace, when people get promoted to a new level, they are often overwhelmed because they are doing their "old job" as well as learning and gaining skill in their new one. Instead of backing away from their old responsibilities so that someone else can pick them up (which makes sense, because those are tasks to be taken over by another person), they continue to focus on staying current with their previous role, retaining mental ownership of it, and neglecting to fully apply themselves to the new tasks of their new role. It can be hard to step away from an area you know so well, but for the sake of your success and your organization's ability to function, it is time to transition your competency focus.

As a coach, when I challenge clients about holding on to the "old job," I frequently hear about the shortcomings of the people who have taken their former position. The conversation usually winds up with some reason the person *has* to keep doing what they used to do in *addition* to their new responsibilities. They say things like, "It's just easier to do it myself," or "This is too complicated for me to explain how to do it right until they hire someone more skilled," or the ever-classic: "We don't have any documentation on it, because I've just taken care of it for all these years, so how am I supposed to dump it on them?"

What is missing here is the distinction between being good at doing a job versus being good at training and mentoring and developing others to do it—or else designing a process by which the work is completed more efficiently and effectively. Why can't someone else be trained on it? Why can't it be documented? Why can't you negotiate time to focus on your new accountabilities? *The skill of managing a role transition is itself a competency, and an essential one for someone who expects to be promoted more than once.* But sticking like glue to what you've already mastered insulates you from building new sets of abilities and competencies. And it prevents others from learning the same way you probably did—from the experience of having to pick up the pieces and figure it out. It isn't difficult to see how falling into such a trap can be career limiting.

Instead, you can become "strategically incompetent" at doing what is no longer your job to do and start focusing on where you need to build competence for your new role. Sure, talk with your replacement about how to do what you used to do, walk them through creating the documentation you never had time to create, but don't go back to doing it yourself! That's the only way you can make room for them to grow, as well as focus on what you need to be developing for your new role. Appreciating others' newfound abilities to fulfill that function, encouraging their recovery from mistakes, and coaching and sharing resources that can help them is now the only relationship you should have with your old job. Get good at *that,* so you can fully take on the new responsibilities and opportunities that come your way in your new position.

The central message of the willingness part of the A-W-S cycle is *we get to choose where to focus our time, attention, and skill building.* There are areas where we don't need to get more skillful because doing so would detract from our goals. Choosing not to develop in those areas protects our focus, energy, and time for the areas where we *are* willing and needing to grow. As the saying goes, "If you can't say 'no,' your 'yes' means nothing." Meaningful work is intrinsically motivating, so focus your attention on what will help you advance the things that are most important to your purpose.

Embracing Your Necessary Stretch

We can't always claim strategic incompetence, though. Consider the following examples of lack of willingness:

» The administrative assistant who backs away from any task or responsibility that is not spelled out in detail, because she is afraid of doing it wrong.

» The consultant who just can't seem to track the details or understand the procedures required for the administrative side of his role. Those who clean up his paperwork messes find his attitude insulting.

» The senior executive who steadfastly refuses to articulate a vision or clarify a strategy, preferring to spend time reviewing and editing others' work.

» The salesperson who remains uninterested in learning a method to track follow-ups and hold herself accountable. She closes sales at an average rate, but could do so much faster.

Each of these individuals is choosing *not* to cultivate willingness to build skills or make changes, and, unlike the first set of examples, this choice is probably not in their best interest.

So how do you discern if the areas you are "choosing not to learn in" are strategic choices or career-limiting ones? *Building your skills and aligning your learning with your strategic priorities keeps you on track.* Calibrate your development investments to support your long-term aspirations and purpose.

For instance, as a business owner, my role requires me to understand the output of an accounting system, but it doesn't require the discipline and procedural knowledge for how to enter the information. That knowledge could be an extra bonus if I had it, but spending my time practicing journal entries is not going to help me build the business. It would only take my time away from the activities that will. However, even though I do not love reviewing financial statements, I do have to understand the reports created from that data to know where we stand. I need to understand the financial view in order to plot our course forward.

A good way to tell if you can afford strategic incompetence in a specific area is to think through the consequences of your *not* learning how to do it. Who would do it then—or should it be done at all? What other options are there to cover the same ground? Will not having that skill limit your future?

Nonstrategic Incompetence

You may want to consider these three patterns of nonperformance that could hinder achieving the successes you seek:

1. **Denial:** There is nothing to learn, there's no problem, and it's not needed. *Denial* is a form of pretense. Denial is resisting change in defense of the status quo. That's a tough way to move forward and grow.

2. **Distraction:** There's too much to do and not enough time to think or focus. We all face a constant deluge of information in our inbox and newsfeed, cell phone texts, and pop-up notifications, and the shifting assignments and pressures of emerging issues for our current projects. People who allow these distractions to overwhelm them can't keep commitments. They overpromise and underdeliver, and they don't track deadlines well because they are overextended. They can't make a conscious choice about where—and where *not*—to focus; they are too distracted.

3. **Dodging:** "It's not my responsibility; someone else is to blame." Ducking accountability and shifting

responsibility to someone or something else raises the likelihood of nonperformance because of displaced culpability. You've probably already heard the blameful tales intended to explain why things aren't working or can't be done. Few organizational environments can avoid them.

If you notice any of these patterns of nonperformance in yourself, you are not alone. We've all engaged in them from time to time. When you find yourself resisting learning, consider it a signal to ensure you are making a strategic choice about what not to learn, or examine if you're shying away from a growth area instead.

Knowing that you have choice about where to focus your time, and taking charge of that decision, allows you to find meaning and fulfillment right where you are, rather than just checking off what others tell you needs to be done. Seeking meaning creates great motivation for learning, so leverage what is meaningful to you.

WHY Do the Reflection Exercises?

» So you will excel at what is most important to you by letting go of what isn't.

» To let others shine at what would have been a distraction to you.

» To release unrealistic expectations.

» So you can learn the best way to be strategically incompetent.

REFLECTION EXERCISES

1. Consider an area of expertise you have held on to, even when
    it was no longer adding much value. What prevents you from
    backing away? Do you feel you have no choice? Start thinking
    through some ways you might be able to "let go" of those areas.

2. Practice saying "no" to one area that you don't want
    responsibility for—personally or professionally. How could you
    lighten your load by renegotiating or removing yourself from
    the project or task in a way that is empowering to others?

3. In what areas are you resisting learning? Are the costs of not
    learning in that area something you can live with long-term?

4. Check for patterns of nonperformance in areas that will limit
    your effectiveness if not addressed.

    Denial
    » Where are you making excuses?
    » Are you using the past as a crutch? (As in, "That's the way
      it's always been done" or "We never needed that before.")
    » Do you resist "burdening others" or exposing a flaw?

    Distracting
    » Are you distracted from focusing on what really matters?
    » How much time do distractions take away from your plans?
    » What are the benefits of distracting yourself? Do they
      outweigh the costs?

    Dodging
    » Are you placing blame on others and their actions when you
      could learn how to be more masterful yourself?
    » Can you pause before you place blame, and make space to
      be more conscious about this as a choice?

5. If you have areas you need to learn about but find draining,
    brainstorm ways to reduce the time you need to spend on
    them. Make them more fun, or reward yourself for taking the
    necessary stretch.

Learning is not a one-time event or a periodic luxury. Great leaders in great companies recognize that the ability to constantly learn, innovate, and improve is vital to their success.

—AMY EDMONDSON
Harvard Business School professor
and author of *Teaming*

PART FOUR

THE SKILL SHIFTS

DEVELOPING *new skills and capabilities* is a strategic response: What does the situation call for? What are we willing to practice and learn to advance our cause?

Problems, opportunities, teamwork, and challenges of all types become a catalyst for growth.

New development happens in ourselves and our skills in response to deliberate practice. Skill building is where the action is. *We drive our learning through doing.*

THE SHIFT:

—FROM—

"How I like to work
and lead is my strength"

—TOWARD—

"Strong leadership adjusts
and grows in service
of a purpose."

18

4D APPLIED LEADERSHIP DEVELOPMENT®

> As a middle manager, of any sort, you are in effect
> a chief executive of an organization yourself. . . .
> As a *micro CEO*, you can improve your own
> and your group's performance and productivity,
> whether or not the rest of the company follows suit.

—ANDREW S. GROVE
Author of *High Output Management*

GARRET WANTED TO BECOME a better leader. He'd come to this small advertising firm a few years prior. They had great potential, good clients, and a solid team. He enjoyed the projects and everyone he worked with, except the founder. The founder, Sydney, was a real challenge. She was opinionated, strong, and brilliant. She had tremendous knowledge of the field and an MBA, but Garret didn't think she could manage her way out of a paper bag. How could she be such a visionary—as many described her— and be flailing and failing to create the business growth and new revenue streams they kept setting as goals? He'd waited two years to see a real change, but it was the "same ol', same ol'" story each month. Garret felt that maybe he should move on (other firms were hiring), because he wasn't sure this company was going anywhere he wanted to go.

Meanwhile, Garret focused on where he felt he could make the most difference: on the projects he oversaw. He enjoyed developing his team and delegating to them with a level of detail and support that they were grateful for. He was proud of his clear, specific instructions. He had long conversations with each staff member about their goals each quarter. He enjoyed the feeling of having personally contributed to some of their successes because of his coaching and sharing of his personal journey. Sydney was not like that at all—people had to sink or swim around her—so he felt he needed to make up for some of the missing care and feeding of the staff by providing more guidance and direction.

When fully understood, the 4D model will change the way you look at leadership growth on the job and give you a clear and workable framework to organize your effort.

When he worked with Sydney, she was always changing things—adding and improving until the last minute—and talking about how the current issue related to the future and the big picture. And then, without any resolution, she was off—pulled away to a phone call and then working intently at her desk until late in the evening. She certainly was prolifically productive. The proposals she wrote (which secured their major clients) were practically works of art, but she was darn confusing to work with. What did she expect people to do? What did she expect from him? No one was quite sure.

For her part, Sydney looked across the office at Garret and wondered whether he was a good fit. He didn't seem to know what to do half the time. His billable hours were too low, and it was hard to get him to move on anything. If she asked him to take out the recycling, he'd probably make a ten-point plan with milestones and checkpoints. She exhaled sharply with disdain for the wastefulness of all these layers being created in her business. On her way back to her office, she shrugged off the thought and moved into client-acquisition mode. Time to buckle down and complete the prep for her next meeting.

Between them, Sydney and Garret illustrate the four key dimensions of Applied Leadership, but individually they are fragmented and unaware of how each of these dimensions is best used. The purpose of the 4D Applied Leadership Model® is to support leaders at all levels, as both a diagnostic and a developmental tool. When fully understood, the 4D model will change the way you look at leadership growth on the job and give you a clear and workable framework to organize your effort. It's easy to learn and remember, although hard to master. It's a model you can continue to apply throughout your career, at any level of seniority.

Here is an overview of the four Ds:

> **Do:** *What is yours to do?* Know and master the requirements of your role.

> **Delegate:** *How can you best engage others to accomplish goals?* Provide clarity and support for others to succeed.

> **Develop:** *Grow the people and processes you need.* Use a growth mindset to discover and develop what is needed to achieve your goals.

> **Design:** *How can you set up for success?* Influence the future with design thinking and a vision. Imagine strategic changes that benefit all involved.

To lead a mission, you'll need all four of these dimensions at different stages and times. You may not be good at all of them to begin with, but growing in each is important if you want to be a better employee and leader. Start where you are, apply what you know, and learn as you grow in the various dimensions that each work situation calls for.

Developing with 4D

Effective top-level leaders build competencies in all four of these areas. They develop flexibility about which skills to draw on for which purposes. They pay attention to what type of leadership is needed and adjust accordingly. When there is an imbalance or overemphasis in one area, or a lack of ability, it becomes a limiting factor in a leader's career growth. Sydney, for example, is focused on the *Design* dimension and the *Doing*. She envisions a future and does a great job with signing on clients and laying out what needs to be done for each. Garret is focused on the *Delegate* and *Develop* dimensions. He carefully assigns responsibilities, provides coaching and mentoring, and builds consistent processes that will allow the company to succeed over time. Neither Sydney nor Garret yet shows understanding or respect for the value in the dimensions they have not yet mastered. Until they mature as leaders who can work together, it will limit their potential and stifle business growth.

When there is an imbalance or overemphasis in one area . . . it becomes a limiting factor.

Leadership matters in the moment. We make choices to lead on a daily basis by applying what we know and increasing our ability to learn more. Knowledge may be interesting in and of itself, but when applied, that knowledge becomes understood and integrated into your leadership style. It becomes knowledge you can use wherever you are, in whatever you are working on, and it's something you grow better at while doing.

Following are specific development suggestions for how to grow yourself to the next level of ability in each dimension.*

Sharpening Your *Do*

How we track, execute, and increase our effectiveness on high-leverage activities, including our daily interactions with others, is the domain of *Do*. Managing your personal work quality, productivity, and focus is a foundation for success, even for skills you haven't developed yet. From setting up the conditions you need to be productive—such as ensuring you have the nutrition, workspace, and equipment to do a good job—to learning and practicing the art of your craft to keeping commitments influences your credibility, capability, and the level of responsibility you earn. Are you able to manage yourself, including your tasks, your strengths, your emotions, reactions, and foibles so you can *do* what's needed to accomplish your work responsibilities and goals?

If you find that staying focused, being productive, or performing with consistently high quality are challenges for you, consider these development options for improving your *Do*:

> » Take charge of your day. Start by noticing how you spend your time. Build awareness of what you intend to do and what actually happens. Reset intentions for higher value and effectiveness and find ways to adjust and compensate for roadblocks and distractions.

---

* In-person and online programs, as well as individual and group coaching offered by Integrated Work, build mastery in these areas. Go to IntegratedWork.com for more details.

» Structure or block time to complete priority tasks, and batch the work so that similar work is grouped together and can be done more efficiently.

» Plan your "Top Three" for each day. Your Top Three are the three items that are your highest priority to accomplish that day.

» Establish supportive work rituals, routines, and processes. Build in recharge time.

» Pick a small skill or habit to improve each month.

Delegation: The Fulcrum of Teamwork

When we work with others or in teams, we coordinate across tasks that are too big to be accomplished by one person. *Delegation* deconstructs projects so they can be successfully completed by the coordinated effort of several people. Delegation demands many specific skills: the ability to parse tasks successfully, clarify goals and subgoals, match the tasks with an individual's capabilities, and track myriad deadlines and interconnecting parts, as well as appreciate the progress being made, even when it's not complete or perfect. The masters of delegation provide clear direction, stay connected to progress, plan for contingencies, and effectively manage multiple projects.

Learning to delegate effectively is an ongoing process of clarifying what is needed, and how each part fits into the larger whole. Here are some areas of development to consider working on in the delegation dimension:

» When looking at your list of priorities, ask, "Who else could be doing this?" Make sure that the tasks and projects you are working on fit your role. If not, is there a person, team, or resource you could delegate to?

» Capture the key components of a project and its deliverables. Build a project plan, even if just for yourself. Create milestones to track progress.

» Figure out the levels of autonomy. Do you or others need to review or approve parts of it? Be clear about what you expect and ensure it is a shared understanding.

» Appreciate good work as it happens. Notes, schwag, or even simple emails are great and simple ways to reward good work.

» Debrief the delegated project or task with those involved to capture the lessons learned and strengthen the process for next time.

Developing People and Processes

We can look at daily issues and challenges, not only from the perspective of the work content, but also for the learning opportunities they provide. How do you develop the skills and abilities of others in your workplace?

Development is an investment in the future. Purpose-driven leaders need a host of on-the-job ways to build their own and their staffs' capabilities *fast*. Challenge one another to grow to the next level, using real-world events as your training ground. How far you *grow* is how far you *go*. Here are some strategies to foster growth as an integrated part of the work week:

> *Challenge one another to grow to the next level, using real-world events as your training ground.*

» Look for stretch assignments for yourself and others, where learning is required to be successful.

Step back, so others can step forward, and then mentor them toward success.

» Designate parts of your day/week/month that are specifically focused on assessing and building the tool sets needed for developing people or processes.

» Have open discussions with those around you, regarding what they are learning and what you are learning. Ask about their aspirations and help them think through the development required to reach them.

» Create feedback loops that show how development activities impact results.

» Reward development gains.

Cultivating Your *Design* Skills

Mastery in the *Design* dimension is one of the hallmarks of an executive. Addressing issues at a strategic level with a future orientation suggests the ability to systemically see how issues interact and interrelate. Awareness of areas of influence, innovation, and transformation increase. Design concepts necessitate the ability to see the big picture—a strategic management perspective that takes into account the intersections between those the organization serves and the health of the internal functional areas that serve them.

Good design connects structure with strategy and leverages the strengths of the organization and its people. Here are some strategies to improve your design skills:

» Develop increased empathy and understanding of those you wish to serve, so you can design solutions that will truly make a difference.

» Seek out diverse perspectives and innovations in other fields and look for patterns or themes across the information you receive.

» Use the tools from Chapter Twenty: "Your Strategic Line of Sight."

» Regularly look for hidden biases and assumptions in your own thinking and challenge them.

» Spend time contemplating your desired future: Formulate and imagine in detail what is important about it and what would make it possible. Think big; create multiple options and multiple futures.

Putting It All Together

Garret met with Sydney to walk through a product launch. Sydney was all over the design aspects and how it would revolutionize their deliverables, but Garret kept returning to the focus of clarifying the objectives for short-term progress, what they needed to do, who would be working on which parts, and how those parts would share information and results. He asked questions and recorded her key thoughts on the conference room whiteboard. By the end of the conversation, Sydney was grateful for the help in putting her dreams into concrete steps. She could see the value of getting these ideas out of her head and having them spelled out for others.

Good design connects structure with strategy and leverages the strengths of the organization and its people.

Over time, she began to develop greater trust and respect for Garret and took an interest in helping him improve his strategic-thinking capacity.

As leaders, we develop our abilities in different dimensions over time, enabling us to master our personal productivity, our management of people and projects, our skills at coaching and mentoring others, and our ability to design new structures and systems to serve our increasing scope of organizational responsibility. Opportunities for development-support exist bidirectionally in most organizations. From any place in the organization, we can look at issues through a growth lens and the corresponding dimension of Applied Leadership required to create that growth.

WHY Do the Reflection Exercises?

» So you can begin putting the 4D Applied Leadership Development model to work for you.

» To clarify where you have the most opportunity for growth and where you are already skilled.

» So you can recognize the strengths and weaknesses of colleagues and those you manage.

» To become a more effective leader and manager of others.

REFLECTION EXERCISES

1. Select a challenge you are currently facing—a messed-up project, a fabulous opportunity, a difficult co-worker, etc. Which dimension—which "D"—of Applied Leadership is really being called for first? How might all the dimensions be applied?

2. If a colleague were to study you when you are at your best, what would they find about the strategies or techniques you use to effectively manage your own workload?

3. What are the most challenging aspects of delegating work to others?

4. If you were to choose one area in which you'd like to develop your staff (or colleagues), what would that be?

5. Is there a process or system missing in your current work environment? How could you work on developing it or learn about what might be more effective than the status quo?

6. In what ways can you contribute to the strategic vision or reenvisioning of your organization? If you imagined starting it over based on what you know now, would it be different? (If you are not the head of a program or department, you may want to look at one of your family's ways of addressing a household management issue like nutrition, vacation, or finances—or consider a community committee, task force, or neighborhood group you are involved with to make working on *Design* something more within your influence.)

THE SHIFT:

—FROM—

"Finding reasons not to listen"

—TOWARD—

"Creating value through generous listening."

19

LISTENING FOR NUGGETS

Listening is not merely not talking, though even
that is beyond most of our powers; it means
taking a vigorous, human interest in what is
being told us. You can listen like a blank wall or
like a splendid auditorium where every sound
comes back fuller and richer.

—ALICE DUER MILLER
American writer and poet (1874–1942)

I RECENTLY BEGAN WORKING again with a client I hadn't
talked to for a few years. She'd just begun a new position, and one
of the first things she did was give me a call. As we caught up on
how things had been going for her, she told me about one of her
current challenges:

> I was only a couple weeks at my new position when
> we had a "meet and greet" with some of the other
> departments. I struck up a conversation with a vice
> president of a different division. Just making conver-
> sation, I asked, "Tell me about your job and how our

two departments connect. How do you see us collaborating to advance the work of your department?" I had no idea what I had just let myself in for. It was like I uncorked a bottle.

The division I stepped into had been leaderless for almost a year, and the relationship between departments had deteriorated. The breakdown of processes from my part of the organization directly impacted her department's workflow and had become a major frustration for her. Collaboration between the divisions was a touchy issue.

For the next ten minutes or so, I just listened and let her emote. Then she laid out four specific examples of how my new division caused angst for her and her staff. Then she said something that really struck me: "I know this work is not important for your department, but we really need to find a way to make it work."

Honestly, Jessica, if you and I had not been over and over listening skills before this, and you hadn't trained me to listen for nuggets in meetings I thought were meaningless, I would have checked out before the first five minutes were up. Instead I was patient and listened hard for what she was really trying to say. When I heard those seven words, "I know this work is not important," I knew I had some new action steps for my team.

"You know what?" I told her, "Your work is important. I heard you say, 'It's not important to your department.' I can already see how if your work can't get done the way you need it to, then my department cannot be successful, because you're basically our gatekeeper to the venues that we need access to. If we don't work well together, we all suffer."

And then it shifted. She looked at me and said, "You know, I haven't heard anyone say something like that in a long time—especially someone who is such a pivotal part of the organization." This woman leads a very logistics-oriented group, and my department is reliant upon that. But it seems clear her division hadn't been receiving what it needed, and this was a tremendous opportunity to do right by all of us by making some positive changes.

What if I didn't know it was important to listen that long? I could have been like, "Yeah, yeah, whatever," and completely missed that insight and opportunity to connect. Without consciously choosing to hear her out, I would've missed that window to build a better, more effective organization, strengthen our collaboration, and reduce everyone's frustration.

The next day, I went to my team and said, "Let's talk about process improvement." I stressed the importance of us working more cohesively with this other group, and it opened up conversation with my team. They said, "We used to do that really well. We know it's fallen apart, and we want to get back on track." Because of that nugget from her, we're all headed in the right direction now.

There are a number of challenges that get in people's way of listening. As this client experienced, the message may come in a package of confrontational, upset, or confused communication. You may dislike or have no respect for the person speaking. People may raise issues in a way you find demeaning or upsetting. In your opinion, they may be boring, arrogant, ignorant, or any one of a thousand other judgments. *None of these judgments matter in relation to your ability to listen for the key points they are making.*

You are responsible for the messages you take in, independent of the speaker's personal characteristics. You may be completely justified in accusing them of glossing over important facts, or of being unfair, domineering, or discriminatory. However, you will not gain any credibility or make progress on the issues unless you can create something more valuable. Just pointing out the problem, or being paralyzed because of it, does nothing to help you, what you care about, or your organization.

People have a deep need to be heard and understood. In workplaces, this is unfortunately rare. Unusually perceptive listening is the basis for increasing our visibility, credibility, and effectiveness. One of the best ways you can move a conversation or meeting forward is to build on points that have been made by others—whether or not you agree with them. When you expand on an idea raised by another person, you acknowledge their contribution and move to a refined version of what they shared. The first step in this process is listening to what the other person is saying, with the intention of finding a valuable nugget to build on.

What if You Disagree?

Most of my clients ask at this point, "But what if I really disagree with what the person is saying?" Listening and understanding a point is different from endorsing it. Whether you agree with a view being expressed or not, the first step is to understand. In fact, you *can't* know if you agree or not until you truly understand what the person is saying. If you can't possibly listen to something you think is flawed and learn from it, you are missing out on a significant human pursuit and source of innovation. Half-baked ideas and opinions can be transformed into breakthroughs after being understood and improved.

Throughout our lives, there will be many things others say with which we will not agree. If the person holding the opinion is an important player in your work or home life, it is indeed useful to understand why they see things as they do. As we mentioned in previous chapters, there is wisdom in multiple perspectives. And how will you gain that wisdom if you don't truly listen to people who see things differently than you do? Hear them out and get curious about what they see that you do not. Relationships continue for a long time and have tremendous power in our lives. Being able to see from another's perspective not only broadens your understanding, but also improves the quality of your relationships, and thus your ability to work together successfully.

Practicing listening at this level has improved my relationships substantially—at work, at home, and in the community. Learning how to appreciate what a loved one is really saying and looking for the nugget I can honor about their communication shifts the whole relationship. When I want to have open communication, personally or professionally, the discipline of listening is the central skill I use.

Real-Time Reflection Questions

Next time you are listening to someone share information at a meeting, ask yourself a few "listening questions" to reflect on in the moment about what they are saying and what it means:

> » **What point has the speaker just made?** This is the
> basis for any further communication on the subject.

Use this question to help yourself pay attention if your mind has wandered. Take notes. Cultivate curiosity about the point, even if you disagree.

» **What is the essence of the issue?** Seek insight into the heart of the matter. What is at the core or root? How can you express this in a simple, objective, and accurate description? Forming and updating different ways you could frame the issue improves your ability to synthesize and express nuanced ideas. You can practice this any time you are listening, even if you are just taking notes. How could this be true? What would make it useful? Out of all of the different angles, which is most critical?

» **Which emotions are being expressed? And why?** Listening for emotion is important because many people make decisions based on how they feel. You need to know if this is a highly charged issue or something more run-of-the-mill. How you respond will change based on the degree and type of emotions expressed by the speaker, yourself, and the others in the room. Connecting with the emotion around a point raised is just as important as connecting with the content. In the example my client shared, she tuned into the emotions of frustration and defeat and realized it was in everyone's best interest to acknowledge and address it.

» **What additional information would the person speaking care about?** This question helps you sort through your own personal databanks to discover if you have any relevant factual information to introduce into the conversation, or if you need to suggest that gathering a particular type of data could shed light on the issue.

» **What have I learned about the situation?** What can you learn from hearing others speak? It may be the process they used, new data about the topic, the politics of the situation, the economics underlying the approach, a different set of beliefs, leverage points, etc. Keep your focus on learning something new rather than defending what you knew before the conversation.

Be generous as you are considering the questions above. Sometimes people fumble with their words, their points may not flow logically, or they may not be graceful in how they share their opinion. Listen for the meaning behind the words. Look for the point they are *trying* to make. Listen for the nugget of gold buried in the muck. If you do not understand what they said, ask a clarifying question or two.

As time allows, you may choose to write down the key points you heard to make them easier to reference. One method I have used successfully for notetaking is to fold your page in half vertically or draw a line down the middle of it. On the left side, I keep track of items others raise. On the right-hand side, I record my thoughts, questions, and reactions.

Be patient with yourself as you practice listening perceptively. As you find yourself slipping into judgment about the speaker—perhaps remembering previous interactions or disengaging for whatever reason—gently return to carefully listening or ask a question. Make a few notes and bring yourself back to the present interaction.

Different Opinions Are a Source of Value

Dialogue and asking great questions are crucial to enlisting the intelligence of a room full of people. What we do with the information obtained can expand our capacity to do more of what matters most. Mutual regard for different perspectives breeds opportunities to learn, go deeper, and gain the benefits of data sources beyond what we already know. We don't attack or damage other people to obtain the value of their perspective; we partner with them.

Holding multiple perspectives is one of the signs of a more mature and more capable mindset. As we become more adept at it, we can see situations from different viewpoints without making one "true" and every other "false." We can see from different vantage points, and we can pick and choose the best aspects of each rather than "throwing the baby out with the bathwater." It also builds respect for colleagues and their backgrounds, and it undermines the dangers of groupthink. Youngsters can't do this—it takes growing up.

As we develop higher orders of mindfulness and awareness, we see more nuance. We realize things aren't so black and white. Time scales elongate, and we can see further. We recognize that an interpretation of what is "right" can change as we learn more—as we understand a bigger picture and a broader context. Some of the things we "know" today will be outdated or updated by a deeper understanding, more information, or a new interpretation tomorrow. Knowledge isn't static.

Holding multiple perspectives is one of the signs of a more mature and more capable mindset.

Decide that you care about uncovering new information, finding new angles, and connecting to new ideas. Leave an interaction with more than you came in with, by deciding to listen, learn, and move your thinking forward.

WHY Do the Reflection Exercises?

» To build awareness of your own listening strengths and areas of growth.

» So you will understand the different ways people listen and have more options.

» So you can leverage what already works for you to be a better listener more of the time.

» To learn to listen well independent of what you are listening to.

REFLECTION EXERCISES

1. Do you know a great listener? How does he or she demonstrate great listening?

2. When you are listening to others, what are you listening for? What do you routinely filter out?

3. How would you rate your performance as a listener at work? In which types of listening situations are you at your best?

4. Do you have different listening habits for different types of coworkers, roles, or situations?

5. What are your barriers to listening?

6. When someone you are listening to holds an opposing viewpoint, how do you respond in the moment? At what point do you stop listening if you disagree? How can you overcome that urge?

THE SHIFT:

—FROM—

"My everyday tasks
aren't that important"

—TOWARD—

"I make my work meaningful
by linking to
bigger-picture goals."

20

YOUR STRATEGIC LINE OF SIGHT

A strategy shouldn't be only a document or
an occasional exercise. It should be a way
of looking at the world, interpreting experience,
and thinking about what a company is and
why it matters. The formal strategic planning
process is only part of it; the deeper
responsibility is ongoing and continuous.

—CYNTHIA MONTGOMERY
Harvard Business School professor
and author of *The Strategist: Be the Leader Your Business Needs*

CHLOE WAS STILL having trouble warming to her new position. In a sense, she still had pretty much the same job as she'd always had, but the organization was growing, and thus her workload. As a result, they'd added three people and made her position a "department," putting her in charge. It felt awkward to tell others to do what she'd always done by herself before, and she didn't want to be seen as coming on too strong—thus the slow thaw.

What she did see as an opportunity, however, was the chance to get ahead of the game for the upcoming CFO Summit that she—er, *her team*—would be organizing this year. There would be about eighty CFOs from various organizations coming together to learn the basics of a new software tool and other new skills, which would be featured in breakout sessions. They were expecting more participants than ever before, and with the extra hands on deck, she could make sure there were fewer surprises—or at least have better systems in place for handling them. She had an upcoming meeting with her team and some of her higher-ups to coordinate the event—and that's where that queasy feeling came in again. She got nervous when she spoke to upper management. She always stopped short of sharing her opinions or recommendations if she felt they wouldn't like them. She'd been taught from an early age to respect authority, but she also knew she wasn't contributing anything if she hid her opinions. Still, she was never quite sure how to share her disagreements in a way that would be well received. She still could feel the sting of her past attempts. They hadn't gone so well and were unpleasant to recall.

Enough of that! She grabbed her planner and turned to the page where she'd recorded her annual goals. She'd set the following two-part learning agenda for herself just a few weeks back:

1. **Improve managing up**

    » Increase willingness and skill in speaking up to those in senior positions, offering value regarding new approaches, and constancy with overall strategic goals.

    » Get more comfortable with making recommendations to senior leaders, including challenging existing approaches. Follow through to see how/if recommendations are acted upon.

2. **Build strength in delegating, teaming, and coaching**

    » Balance needs for quality control and ownership with effective utilization of the other staff members available to support training and learning projects.

    » Implement several successful training projects this year—with a lighter workload because the ownership and deliverables are shared.

Designing and delivering training is where she felt most comfortable, so she was glad that this foray into team leadership was on her home turf.

Critical Success Factors

Chloe considered what was most important about this CFO Summit, beyond getting it completed with satisfied participants. From the perspective of the senior leadership, she imagined that they would want positive buzz among the CFOs, talking about how this summit was valuable to them. She also knew there was a larger directive to take better advantage of technology and build greater technical expertise into each training. Since this summit did have a new software tool being introduced, maybe making a bit of progress on increasing modernization would also connect to the strategic perspective.

As for the participants, she knew they would want to have time for networking and sharing with their peers between each session. This was great because those relationships helped engage people and accelerate their learning. It was also part of their mission to build a strong network of colleagues across the country, so she could definitely see how unstructured time was important.

Chloe's objectives going into the planning meeting with her team were to outline a project plan and make assignments. However, as she thought it through, she realized that unless she connected everyone involved to the larger context for the summit, they probably wouldn't see it for themselves. This would affect the way they approached their parts. Plus, they might see things she didn't about how to leverage the summit to better accomplish those strategic goals, so she decided to put the big-picture discussion right at the top of the planning-meeting agenda.

CFO Summit Team Kickoff Meeting Agenda

» Overall purpose of the summit

» Connections to strategic objectives

» Leveraging this event to make short-term progress on longer-term goals

» Lessons learned from previous summits

» Outline of project plan

» Next steps

In years past, she might have started with the "Outline of the project plan," but she had learned how much more influence she could have and how it helped everyone be better aligned if she led everyone to the big goals first. If she started with a discussion of the overall purpose—the "why" behind the event—she could be sure everyone was on the same page from the beginning. Plus, seeing the bigger picture infuses meaning into everyday work.

Without realizing it, the queasy feeling had turned into a tingle of anticipation. She wondered what she might learn with all of these other voices in the room. It was going to be nice to have some help. Who knew what they might come up with together?

Everyday Events of Strategic Importance

Being strategic isn't isolated to planning retreats, SWOT (Strengths, Weaknesses, Opportunities, Threats) analyses, or annual meetings. Every day we can choose to connect our immediate, tactical work to a larger picture—and advance both. By linking our day-to-day with the larger picture, we consciously create short-term progress on long-term objectives. This inspires greater satisfaction and meaning in the work itself, and it produces better results.

Each time we step back from the tactical, and practice making the connection between daily events and strategic goals, we open up the possibility of addressing several objectives through single actions. When Chloe stopped to figure out how she could use a simple planning meeting to further her learning goals, she also discovered ways to support the company's strategic objectives and create action steps that would multiply the effects with a more thorough planning approach.

Even though predicting the future is impossible, we can learn a lot from talking through how things *might* unfold and walking through different scenarios. If you do this in a group, you will notice the brilliance of diversity and the value of having people in the room who think and see differently than you. *Seeing issues from multiple perspectives is the superpower of our time.*

The sparks of insight that burst forth from future-planning conversations can change the trajectory of a career, a cause, and/or an organization. What is most important about these conversations is that they illustrate that there are more possibilities than we realized. Our imaginations are a critical tool to our success. Focusing that imagination in thought experiments that reveal new layers of understanding, or forge new paths of possibility, creates tremendous value without the cost associated with trial and error. And you can do this type of thinking for yourself, using the every-day events, projects, and assignments given you. Practicing doing this work on daily events prepares you, strengthens you, and builds your capability for strategic leadership at work, at home, and in your community.

How different will Chloe's meeting be because she's starting from the strategic perspective rather than from the project-planning perspective? How differently might a project you are working on turn out if you start by investing time in strategic thinking?

The situations we are in, the data we consider, the things people say to us, and the problems that show up on our doorstep can all be dealt with at different levels. The key variable is how you interpret the circumstance. Most people don't consciously choose the level at which to address issues; they just react. By thinking ahead and attempting to influence the future through your actions, you create a convergence between strategic thinking, your daily activities, and who you are becoming through their convergence.

Strategic Line of Sight

The diagram on the next page illustrates how everyday experiences can relate to your larger mission and purpose. Personal vision is what you are trying to accomplish. Strategies are the thoughtful choices you make about your actions as you pursue that vision. Events are the activities you take part in every day. Connecting the dots between these different levels is the strategic line of sight between everyday events and what matters most.

The Big, Big Picture

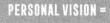 **PERSONAL VISION =** What you want; the future you desire.

STRATEGIES = Methods to get closer to your vision.

EVENTS = What you do to make things happen.

Your Daily Experiences

You may notice that the arrows show movement in both directions—up *and* down. This is because personal strategic planning is an ongoing creative process. Most of us have seen the flow from vision to strategy to event—a top-down approach. However, visions and strategies are also affected by daily events. For example, one day you may have a deep talk with a colleague that influences a decision to go back to school, apply for a management position, or take better care of yourself. This conversation may lead you to think through new approaches or strategies for how to achieve what you want in life. Having this conversation helps clarify and refine your vision.

Leaders who are prompted to think strategically based on everyday events have many opportunities to use their line of sight to accomplish important objectives, devise ways to get things done in the short-term, and make long-term progress with each task, moving in a reinforcing direction.

Another way to approach this is to ask yourself, "What Win Works?" Each word represents a question that will help you be strategic in day-to-day decisions:

> **What:** What overall objectives does this situation connect to?

> **Win:** What potential learning, gain, or progress could this situation provide?

> **Works:** How do I integrate this with what matters most?

Consciously choosing the level at which to address the issues and opportunities that come your way, and seeing the connections along the strategic line of sight, increase the likelihood that you will recognize how to use the activities you take part in every day for your growth and development. This creative interplay between daily events and the big picture refines the art of living on purpose.

WHY Do the Reflection Exercises?

» To connect your work to a bigger-picture mission.

» To increase the meaning of day-to-day work through strategic goals.

» So you will feel inspired and valued more regularly.

» To practice creating a "Strategic Line of Sight."

REFLECTION EXERCISES

Every day we make decisions—about how to spend our time, what to say, whom to call on, when to take action, and when not to. Those choices are either consistent or inconsistent with our organization's and our own personal goals. Here are some ways to link daily work to bigger-picture goals.

1. Identify a tasks or project you are working on that you care about but seems disconnected from the mission. What priorities does your organization have that this might relate to?

2. List three ways this task might serve the bigger picture and thus become more meaningful.

3. Could you ask others in your workplace for their perspective on how the current work connects to the overall organizational mission? Is there an opportunity to identify a win that works for all involved?

4. What meeting do you attend that would benefit from a stronger connection to the strategic line of sight? How could you help clarify the purpose for all involved?

5. Pretend that a senior leader showed up at your desk and asked you how the particular task you were doing connected to the mission of the company. What would you say?

6. What information are you learning from day-to-day experiences that might refine or change the big-picture strategic vision?

THE SHIFT:

—FROM—

"Others make the decisions
about my work"

—TOWARD—

"I can influence
how things work out."

21

THE ART OF LEADING UP

When the whole world is silent,
even one voice becomes powerful.[21]

—MALALA YOUSAFZAI

Pakistani teen who survived being shot by the Taliban
and Nobel Prize laureate

"I'M REALLY GOOD at making mountains out of molehills."

The interviewer's eyes widened.

Sheila suppressed a sly smile. She knew that wasn't a typical answer to the typical question, "What strengths would you bring to our team?" She wasn't trying to be flippant. She really wanted this position, and she also wanted to let her interviewer know she wasn't a run-of-the-mill candidate.

"Let me explain," she continued.

Her interviewer nodded.

"Small indicators and changes in the environment are sometimes early signs of a larger trend, so extrapolating on what they might become, if magnified, yields insights that have a lot of benefits. Such insights show us where to innovate. In my past positions, it's something I've found I have a knack for. Looking at those potential trends, I always ask myself, 'What mountain could this molehill turn into?' This question leads to higher-level problem solving and a more systemic, forward-thinking viewpoint. Just because an event is small doesn't mean there aren't strategic implications."

Sheila noted the interviewer's interest and continued to explain, "When I wrap those strategic implications into a compelling story, data point, or set of trends—something that gives them context—my managers and team members can see how they relate to implementing a strategy or issue that is weighing on us. Communicating from this perspective, outward and upward, means I gather business intelligence by scanning the environment. I find early warning signs. Then I test to see if it is an emerging trend our organization needs to address. That's how I have found that my strength for making mountains out of molehills actually benefits everyone I work with."

Sheila's breath caught in her throat. When her interviewer's face went from puzzlement to a smile, she found she could breathe again.

"That's the first time I've heard that one," the interviewer said, nodding. He made a note on his tablet.

Sheila released the tension in her shoulders. *I got this*, she told herself.

Leading Your Leaders

Over her career, Sheila had built the skill of using strategic extrapolation to think through implications, test different explanations, and look for patterns to distinguish indicators others were likely overlooking. That insight was useful information for her managers. When her insights were relevant to the organization's direction and needs, it could open the door to pivotal new approaches.

It's one thing to communicate to your team and peers, but quite another to make sure your strengths have impact "up the chain of command" as well. Sheila is one of many we've had the opportunity to coach on the fine art of "managing up."

Each type of manager offers opportunities for developing new masteries in not only leading up, but also in leading forward.

Managerial styles vary. Some managers won't give you the time of day; some won't leave you alone. Some are terrible at details; others lack an understanding of the big picture. Some are too new to know anything; others rely too much on their experience to be current. Unpredictable bosses are some of the most challenging. Each type of manager offers opportunities for developing new masteries in not only leading up, but also in leading forward.

Here are a few other things to keep in mind as you seek to connect with the authorities in your world in a way that will benefit them, increase the impact of your strengths, and ultimately increase your contribution overall.

1. Learn what is important to your manager.

What are your manager's priorities? What do they care about and want to focus on or talk about? By taking a proactive approach to the relationship and knowing what they care about, you can help them be more effective by aligning with what you're doing right. Observe and ask questions. If there are documents that reference strategic priorities, read them. Discuss how your role fits within the company priorities and what your manager considers most important for the next few months. Generally, managers are glad to have an employee who is curious about organizational priorities and interested in working in alignment with them.

You do not have to be in charge in order to lead. In fact, more and more companies are actually looking for better ways to capture honest upward communication of information or ideas that directly impact what they care about.

2. Don't make more work for your manager.

When you send an email or are asking about a next step in an assignment, word things to provide an idea or solution to which your manager can simply respond "yes" or "no." Do not ask questions like "What should I do about X?" Questions like that put the burden of creating and thinking through the options solely on your manager. If she has to think it all through, what good are you? Look for ways to add value. Ask your manager how you can be of greater support. To do this, you can use prompts like "I'm considering. . ." or "I plan on . . ." or "We could . . ."*

If you want to be trusted to make good decisions, you have to show you can think things through. One way to show you are engaged is to share your opinion in a helpful way, such as: "Between options A, B, and C, I think C is best because . . ." Or you could identify the steps needed to move forward, such as: "To determine the best approach, we could . . ." Depending on the level of trust you have created, you might then either ask for approval, such as "Let me know if I should proceed with Option C" or communicate intent: "Unless I hear from you, I will move forward with Option C."

---

* For more on this idea, see David Marquet's chapter "I Intend To . . ." in his book *Turn the Ship Around!: How to Create Leadership at Every Level* (Austin, TX; Greenleaf Book Group Press, 2012), 84-91.

3. Practice good conversational hygiene.

Clean your exchanges of subtle digs, flare-ups over small issues, and "he said/she said" drama. Be someone who de-escalates situations, clarifies what is needed, and helps decisions get made. Spooling up blame, defensiveness, or unproductive behaviors will only detract from your success. Figure out what you can do to help instead.

If you want your managers to listen to you, connect with what they care about. Help them see how what you are talking about benefits the areas they are focused on. Connect the dots to show specifically how your work, or the issue you want to raise or resolve, advances the organization's priorities. If you're unsure of the priorities, circle back and find out what they are.

4. Demonstrate your value.

Reliably deliver what is expected from your role, and communicate that progress. Focus on the highest-priority work. Ensure that your contribution to the organization exceeds your cost. Regularly reflect on how you can enhance your value and improve your performance. How can you keep those higher up informed of what you are doing?

Right here is where a lot of people run into internal resistance: "I can't share what I've been doing proactively; that would be like bragging! I'm not that type of person." That's a refrain I've heard many times. Who do you think is more likely to get recognition?

A. The people who share what they are doing so that others know about it, or

B. Those who wait for someone to notice the great work they have been doing?

Right. So if you refuse to share what value you are creating, then live with the fact that you decrease the likelihood of recognition for it. If you want recognition, then get better at helping other people to see the value of what you do. Of course, sharing information about what you are doing can be done gracefully, without bragging. Start by providing an update on accomplished projects or factual results from your or your team's efforts. Communicate the relevant information so there is an opportunity for others to be aware.

You can think about it as a corollary to the "no surprise" policy. If you have been doing great work, isn't it just as important to let a manager know as it is to let her or him know there's a big problem? The overall key is to practice regular, proactive communication geared to the level of detail your manager prefers. If you are anticipating something good or bad, share the evidence and why you think it's important that others know about it.

5. Can you appreciate your manager?

Not everyone is a great manager. To me, it's a sacred duty to be a leader who inspires, grows, and develops employees to be authentic, human, and high performing, but that's rare. Most of us bumble along trying to find the balance between hard and soft feedback, patience or pressure, when to direct and when to coach.

Even though your manager might do things you don't like, it's more likely she's just not great at being a manager *yet* (remember "the power of yet"?) than it is she is diabolically plotting to undermine you at every encounter. We're all human. Sometimes managers make mistakes and they learn how to get better at what they do as a result, just like you and me. At the same time, they are probably doing wonderful things you don't notice because they are not front and center for you, any more than you are for them. There should be an ongoing process of forgiving, learning, and moving forward on both sides. Perhaps managing *you* is not as easy as it should be. After all, you know what you need, but how would your manager? Appreciate that you and your manager may both be great people looking at the same situation from different vantage points. Help bridge the gaps through communication. Growing is a two-way street. So is recognition. Mutual positional empathy is a great mindset to start from.

> *Appreciate that you and your manager may both be great people looking at the same situation from different vantage points. Help bridge the gaps through communication.*

When managers provide you resources or suggestions, thank them. Use positive feedback to let them know what works well for you. Who knows, you might get more of it. Accept mentoring and advice, even if you are not sure you want it. You may not agree with, or always value, their opinion, but see what you can learn from it and appreciate that they took the time to share their thoughts with you.

6. When your manager is wrong.

For many mission-driven leaders, being critical of their bosses happens because they recognize things they could be doing better, or perhaps things they shouldn't be doing at all. This is a good indicator of your leadership potential, but it doesn't mean that you're right about everything you think or that you're ready to take your manager's place. It means you are a strategic, forward-thinking employee who looks at how to lead toward a better future. That is a huge leverage point for you, but it can also be a downfall if it turns out you don't know how to keep things positive. How can you best use what you see for your department? How can you communicate it in a way that will be beneficial? Are you open to being wrong? What if your manager knows something you don't? (Which she or he usually does.)

7. Address issues directly and professionally.

In extreme instances (illegal activities, substance abuse, or mental illness), you might need to go over a manager's head, but such circumstances are rare. It takes courage to speak to your manager directly and clearly about how you see things and where you can have the best impact in your work. How you raise issues says a lot about you as a professional.

Practice reflecting and writing issues out, avoiding the emotion and identifying the most important information. Rewrite your points and then communicate the facts as you see them, along with your interpretation of what those facts imply.

If you are fortunate and have worked through these tips, your manager will communicate directly with you, building a solid, trusting, and collaborative relationship. As the old saying goes, "It takes two to tango." The quality of your relationships up the career ladder are just as much in your hands as anyone else's. Be a solid, reliable colleague in all directions.

Do the Reflection Exercises?

» To identify the skills to effectively "manage up."

» To improve your ability to influence through better communication.

» So you can adjust your approach to get better results.

» To create more trusting, professional, and collaborative relationships.

REFLECTION EXERCISES

1. What is something you think could be improved or handled better at your company? Can you imagine multiple solutions and recommendations to improve it? Craft at least three ideas you could share.

2. What do you notice about those who are able to successfully "manage up" in your organization? How do they wield influence?

3. Can you connect the improvement you have identified to what leadership cares about? How can you prepare to discuss these issues professionally, and without drama?

4. How often do you communicate appreciation or gratitude to your manager or leadership? When was the last time you told your manager about something they did that worked well for you?

5. Are you open to feedback and revisions to your proposed solutions? Can you partner with others to design even better responses to this issue?

6. What is your next area for learning in the art of "managing up"?

THE SHIFT:

—FROM—

"Being painted into a corner
of overcommitment"

—TOWARD—

"Proactively developing a solution
to the satisfaction of all."

GRACEFUL RENEGOTIATION

Attachment to praise and avoidance of criticism
keeps us from doing innovative, controversial
work and—more simply—from following the paths
we feel called toward, whether or not those around
us understand or approve.

—TARA MOHR

Author of *Playing Big: Practical Wisdom for Women
Who Want to Speak Up, Create, and Lead*

FOR BUSY PROFESSIONALS, times always come when we
cannot do what we originally thought we could. When unexpected
events arise, or we exceed our personal limits, we need to recon-
sider our commitments. Sometimes, creative approaches make
it possible to manage an overflowing workload, but, more often,
we need to be ready to renegotiate our workload to preserve our
professional and personal integrity. Consider these examples:

Jenny agonized from the moment she woke on Saturday morning. Torn between going to her son's basketball tournament and
outlining the research project her client expected to review on
Monday, she felt split in two. Her heart sank. To compromise her

relationship with her son or disappoint an important client wasn't a choice she ever wanted to make.

Mark committed to have the software fix ready this week. By Thursday afternoon it was painfully clear the problem would not be fixed for another two weeks. How is he going to break the news without losing credibility?

At the request of one of her organization's board members, Darlene took on several important projects. As a result, other critical work was falling behind. Mapping out the remaining tasks, she saw no way to complete all her responsibilities on time. The sense of failure was overwhelming and depressing. How did she get herself into this? And what could she do now?

Gracefully handling difficult communications that adjust and/or clarify expectations demonstrates how our deepest values are applied in the workplaces.

Gracefully handling difficult communications that adjust and/or clarify expectations demonstrates how our deepest values are applied in the workplace. The very complex process of evaluating your priorities, capabilities, and commitments can take different forms. However you choose to approach the process, consider the following steps on your way to gracefully renegotiating your situation so that all parties remain connected and able to move forward.

1. Connect to the broader context.

Take a step back from the urgent. In order to gather your thoughts to respond well, you'll need a little mental space to reflect. Consider: *What is the larger system in which this particular event exists?* Any one promise is usually nested within several layers of commitments, which leaves you with considerable options for renegotiation.

For instance, Jenny could be looking at renegotiating family responsibilities with her spouse, or the way she ended up with the research project in addition to her regular workload, or the time frame that someone else in the firm determined without checking the capacity of her team. Options for renegotiation can be addressed in any or all of those layers. From this larger context, Jenny's feelings of being trapped may evaporate as she sees different work-arounds and where she has choices. Sometimes renegotiation can actually make the situation better for everyone by examining the underlying issues and having an honest, constructive conversation about what really matters and what can be done differently moving forward.

If you need space to determine your layers, try one or more of the following:

» Take a walk, get a cup of coffee, or go somewhere you can think clearly, someplace "outside the conflict zone."

» Narrate the situation as if you were describing the story line of a movie about someone else. What is the context for the conflict? Try variations of the story to find one that is valuable as a framework for how this situation was created.

» Consider others you have known in similar situations. How is your context different? Compare and contrast to help illuminate your situation.

» Ask a friend, trusted advisor, or coach to help you see the different components of this situation.

2. Identify the real need.

Some people are reluctant to realize when a change is needed. They continue to uphold awkward and painful agreements long after they could have been renegotiated. The challenge may have snuck up in small increments, and now they are culminating in a need for change.

At this stage, it is important to come to terms with what is authentically working and not working for you. This is the time to jettison notions that others' needs are also your needs. Instead, look into the heart of the matter and ask yourself the following questions:

- » What is not working?

- » How important is it, really?

- » What *really* needs to be done, and when? Is there room for adjustment?

- » What aspects are working and need to be preserved?

- » What can change? How should those things change?

3. Cultivate understanding of other people's perspectives.

A successful renegotiation leaves all parties respected and clear on how to proceed and what to expect. To be effective, it is useful to understand what is important to other people—their goals, aspirations, and concerns—so that you can connect with their purposes and respect them. You will find that gathering information is important at this stage. Consider what you know about the others involved and how you can preserve what is most important to them while changes are under way.

Darlene, for instance, was contemplating the balance between what the board asked her for and the other projects that were already on her plate. After realizing it was impossible to do it all, she felt she needed more information about the priorities in order to analyze the impact of each project being done on time or not. She mapped out what she thought the board member was after, and the impact on her management team if she didn't complete their part. She identified three easy things she could do to move the requested projects forward and decided to check to see if this would meet the board member's needs in the short-term. He was usually easy to reach via email, so Darlene outlined her approach in an "I intend to . . ." email and let the board member know she could adjust if he had concerns or questions.

> *To be effective, it is useful to understand what is important to other people—their goals, aspirations, and concerns—so that you can connect with their purposes and respect them.*

His response? "Sounds good."

What a relief!

4. Generate options.

Your situation may require more than a clarification like Darlene's. In that case, it is helpful to create a range of options from which to choose. The first two options that usually occur to us—do what we agreed or disappoint others—are not the only ones, nor are they likely to be the best.

For Mark, the reasons the software fix wouldn't be completed on time were complex. He had a long list of things that were still not working. But what *really* mattered? This software fix was important because a group that needed to process their data was waiting for it. Two weeks would be a long time for them to wait, and there was virtually no way he could get a production release of the code before then. So what other options did he have? Maybe he could decouple these two competing issues by finding a short-term way to get the data processed for the group, which would eliminate the time crunch for the software. He stood up and looked around for Chad. Chad would know how to get a quick data run in without disrupting the programmers. Once he found Chad and worked out the details, he proposed this option for getting the immediate need met. At the same time, he informed management of the longer time frame needed for the software fix.

In today's fast-paced world, we can often find ourselves in unproductive conversations because both parties are jumping to conclusions based on misinterpretations or assumptions.

Consider the following questions to help you generate more options. You may choose to organize what you come up with into a continuum, from one extreme to the other, in order to find a point along the way that feels like the best move.

> » What would you normally do in a situation like this? What is the opposite of what you would normally do?

> » What would a leader whom you admire consider doing?

> » What have you always wanted to do, but never thought you could?

» What are the safest options? What are the riskiest?

» How do other industries, or co-workers, handle similar issues?

5. Respect yourself by preparing.

A successful renegotiation is best done when you are calm, relaxed, and clear about what is most important to you. Save emotional outpourings for another setting. Create the space you are comfortable functioning in by selecting the meeting time and location. Prepare notes on the options you will propose, if you need them, and your alternatives if your initial proposals are not accepted.

Knowing you are prepared, you can allow yourself to be present in the moment and be attentive to what is happening during the renegotiation. Listen to what the other person needs so you home in on the options that will work best for you both. This added awareness is a powerful ally in creating solutions. This allows you to cocreate with the other person, often coming up with an option that meets everyone's needs better than what you came up with alone.

6. Begin where you are right now.

Before offering potential solutions, frame the situation as you understand it. Describe the larger picture, what you want to change, and what you see as important to the other parties involved. Express what you want to do and what you need others to do. Do not spend time justifying what you need or want. Just ask for it. If questioned about your reasons, explain then.

In today's fast-paced world, we can often find ourselves in unproductive conversations because both parties are jumping to conclusions based on misinterpretations or assumptions. Grounding your discussion in the present before you get too far into suggesting options can save a lot of time, energy, and emotional capital.

7. Clarify your reasoning.

There is risk in renegotiating a deal, just as there is risk in not renegotiating. What if they don't agree? In their book, *Getting to Yes*, Roger Fisher and William Ury speak of the BATNA—Best Alternative to a Negotiated Agreement.[22] What will you do if they're not willing to renegotiate? Having thought this through is incredibly useful for clarifying what you are willing to risk to create something better. Knowing you have at least one alternative gives you freedom in any negotiation.

Push-back during a discussion does not mean that your request to renegotiate is being rejected. You may need to explore and ask questions to determine what really matters to the other parties and how all parties needs can be met.

When we are talking only to ourselves, we probably don't have enough information. Consider writing out your reasoning for renegotiating to clarify your thoughts, organizing your points in a way that would be accessible to someone else. Ask yourself:

» If you were to consider yourself an outside party in this situation, looking after the mutual interests of all involved, does your reasoning hold up?

» Is your renegotiated solution fairer than, or as fair as, the existing arrangements?

» What are your most important reasons for this renegotiation?

» Is there a thinking partner or advisor you might share this with to help you analyze the implications and approach you want to present?

8. Be prepared for disagreement.

Push-back during a discussion does not mean that your request to renegotiate is being rejected. You may need to explore and ask questions to determine what really matters to the other parties and how all parties needs can be met. Acknowledge their objections: "I understand where you are coming from, and I hope you can see that the present arrangements just aren't feasible. What can we work out?" Be firm, direct, and push forward to a solution that works for everyone.

9. Agree on action items.

What needs to happen now so that you don't have to renegotiate later? Track and confirm who will do what and by when. If you use a task or project management app or software, treat what you work out together as a new project so you can track the details and dates closely. Carefully note the agreed-upon action items and due dates. Before you leave, make sure you've answered these questions:

» What outcomes are these negotiated changes designed to accomplish? (It is useful to gain agreement on this as a basis for action.)

» What short-term actions will move the situation closer to the desired outcome?

» What additional actions will be needed down the road?

» When will you revisit this to discuss how these changes are working out?

10. Appreciate.

Recognize that you found a creative way to address a difficult situation and thank those who accommodated your needs and helped you find a solution. Appreciation can take many forms. A simple and sincere "thank you" works for most. (If you feel something more involved would be appropriate, see Chapter Twenty-Three on appreciation.)

WHY Do the Reflection Exercises?

» To identify and remove roadblocks to successful renegotiation.

» To change any negative perspectives on renegotiation you may have.

» To more fully recognize how others successfully renegotiate with you.

» So you can assess your renegotiation skills and identify areas for improvement.

REFLECTION EXERCISES

1. What holds you back from renegotiating a situation at work or in ife? Does this prevent you from even considering or exploring more realistic or fair expectations? How has renegotiating unsuccessfully hurt you in the past?

2. Think of a time someone had the courage to renegotiate a deal, deadline, or commitment with you that either didn't bother you, or maybe even benefited, you?

3. What did you notice about the skills they used to negotiate successfully? Did they offer multiple solutions, communicate with respect, understand your perspective, confirm your real need, or something else? Which of these skills come naturally to you?

4. Is there a situation in work or life where you presently feel overcommitted? Is there a part of this situation that, if renegotiated, could provide a relief or better outcome for you?

5. What are the potential risks of renegotiating? Do the risks of renegotiating outweigh the consequences of leaving things as they are?

6. Imagine yourself on the other side of this situation, having found a good way through it. What does it feel like to have overcome it? Let appreciation and gratitude for yourself and others emerge. How have you grown through the experience? Now that you've visualized that end, how do you get there?

THE SHIFT:

"Feeling undervalued
and unappreciated"

"Skillfully acknowledging
the value of myself and others."

23

THE PRACTICE OF APPRECIATION

Remember, it's not just workers but souls
who are gathered in the workplace;
we're not just here to "achieve" in a worldly sense,
but to spiritually grow. . . .
Ultimately, it's only people who have done
and continue to do their own inner work
who can effectively lead a competent
modern workplace.

—MARIANNE WILLIAMSON
Author of *Everyday Grace*

FOR THE THOUSANDTH TIME, Greta took a deep breath in and let it out with a heavy, long sigh. *Here we go again.*

"There is *no* appreciation for what I do!" she exclaimed.

Greta worked with a team of clinical specialists, and she provided their program management support—which meant she saved their butts regularly—and apparently, they either didn't know or didn't care.

Greta's work experience was tainted by the resentment of feeling personally undervalued and by the lack of others' caring about what mattered for her role. However, if she wasn't around exactly when they needed her, or if she was busy with another project, then they cared and showed their displeasure, because they needed what she provided *right now.* It required a lot of skill to do her work correctly, and when they had to wait for those skills, their projects were at a standstill. Maybe they were being jerks and deliberately causing crises, or maybe it just worked out that way, but it didn't matter. The anger and angst it caused Greta were making her work life miserable, even though she was great at her job and tremendously enjoyed the work itself.

Her mentor suggested Greta experiment with making a couple of changes. She was willing to try anything.

First, she created a visible display of existing work projects on her office whiteboard, where she showed everyone who came by exactly which programs had which status and what the next action steps were for each. People could stop by her office and look across all of the programs for updates, instead of needing to interrupt her to ask where their project stood. She liked that her attempt to be more transparent about her workload had the added benefit of seamlessly answering these questions. She never realized such a small change could have so much impact.

When a new clinical administrator was hired, he began coming by to discuss the priority of programs, links between the programs, and current strategies being used. He also opened up to her about how the company was responding to market pressures. Being in on this kind of higher-level conversation was particularly rewarding for Greta. She aspired to be able to lead more advanced projects and wanted to build a greater ability to influence. These meetings felt like customized leadership training sessions.

The second change Greta adopted was to more openly communicate successes. She was one who had always been uncomfortable with what she referred to as "tooting her own horn." She didn't want others to think she was arrogant, claiming unwarranted credit, or grandstanding. However, she had swung the pendulum of potential communication from bragging to the other extreme: literally hiding her contributions.

There are many options in between those two extremes. You can share successes without being annoyingly self-promoting, and it is useful to your company and co-workers to know what is working for you. That allows them to focus more on the things that contribute positively and less on the stuff that doesn't. Whatever one's role, knowing what works, paying attention to what gets good results and what is effective means orienting to high-quality performance that builds toward success—all very good things.

As she communicated with her co-workers about the things she was proud of contributing to and shared more about her processes, Greta's resentment began to melt away. She was asked to give a presentation on what she did as part of employee orientation so that new teammates could understand the issues she faced and how to partner with her to achieve the best results. Their rapt attention as she spoke bolstered her confidence and love for what she did.

Whatever one's role, knowing what works, paying attention to what gets good results and what is effective means orienting to high-quality performance that builds toward success—all very good things.

These two relatively small changes set in motion a series of events that transformed Greta's career. Where she previously felt like an undervalued, underappreciated, lower-level employee, she now felt like an integral part of her company.

Less than a year after she started coaching, Greta was promoted to become a manager of managers, directing and delivering on cutting-edge projects, exactly what she had hoped to do with her career when she started. Where she had previously been stalled, she was now advancing, and it was her work that propelled her forward.

Are you being compassionate and encouraging with yourself as you learn, make mistakes, and try new approaches?

Her experiments in doing things differently quickly shifted how she saw herself. She now saw where she fit into the whole from a strategic perspective. This helped her recognize how she could positively impact her situation, provide more value and support to her co-workers, and ultimately influence the growth of her organization.

Appreciation Starts with You

When you need to feel more appreciated in your role, the first step is to appreciate yourself. How does what you do add value to those around you? Get crystal clear about the specifics. Working hard is not the same as adding value. Instead, ask yourself what is the result or impact of your hard work? Does it save time, produce something, satisfy a customer, align departments, avoid expenses, or accelerate a process? In what ways do you create value greater than the cost of your First Paycheck and benefits? Do others understand the value you provide? How can you show them? How can you make it visible in a way that helps others be better at what they do? If you were appreciating your own work, what would you be doing differently?

According to research on positive psychology in the workplace, the number-one reason most Americans leave their jobs is that they don't feel appreciated. In fact, "65 percent of Americans reported receiving no recognition for good work last year."23 This is such an important factor in work satisfaction. Don't leave it up to someone else! Learn to appreciate yourself so you have recognition from at least one person. Then you can influence outward and upward from there.

You may also want to pay attention to how you treat yourself. Are you being kind to yourself? Do you set appropriate boundaries? Do you take good care of your well-being? Do you give yourself a reward when you've done something great—even if it's just acknowledging a small triumph? Mature, conscious professionals monitor what they need in order to feel whole in their work and then make certain they get it. Are you being compassionate and encouraging with yourself as you learn, make mistakes, and try new approaches? Being supportive of yourself is the first step to engaging others' support and being genuinely and generously able to appreciate others.

When examining beliefs around appreciation, gratitude, and recognition, some people find they have simply never felt comfortable acknowledging themselves for their success. This discomfort limits their ability to feel appreciated, because they discount their success and then expect others to see them and treat them as more valuable than they are willing to see themselves. The internal work of appreciating oneself often leads

> When you appreciate others, it shows you acknowledge the value of their contribution and believe in their potential.

to a shift in perspective that others notice. It's much different than bragging. It's self-confidence and self-recognition that make room for others to join in.

Demonstrating Appreciation

If you are a manager or want to become one, it is especially useful for you to consider your individual journey and your beliefs about appreciation in the workplace. Clean up any outdated beliefs impacting your work. Some believe they shouldn't have to show appreciation for others' contributions; others mistakenly believe that acknowledging success means people will stop working so hard. In fact, lack of appreciation diminishes others' enthusiasm to contribute and discourages talented people. Everyone wants to feel competent and valued, which is exactly what showing them appreciation does.

The power of appreciation is profound. Knowing that others see us, appreciate us, and wish to encourage us matters. To *appreciate* means "to grasp the nature, worth, quality, or significance of" and "to increase in ... value."[24] When you appreciate others, it shows you acknowledge the value of their contribution and believe in their potential. And it increases their sense of worth and therefore, personal investment in shared goals.

While many individuals appreciate being recognized publicly, others find it awkward. For some, a handwritten note really hits the spot; for others, a small gift or treat would be well received. Some appreciations are monetary; others provide new opportunities, challenges, or exciting assignments. Some people just want some downtime. There are hundreds of ways to appreciate staff and co-workers, and you may want to experiment with a variety of methods to find what works best for different people.

Here are some less common strategies to consider in addition to the traditional thank-you notes, verbal recognition in front of peers, company awards, certificates, and bonuses:

THE PRACTICE OF APPRECIATION

For Appreciating Yourself

1. **New opportunities.** What professional development
    would help you move forward and grow the value
    you can deliver? Start investigating programs, books,
    classes, blogs, people, or groups that know about the
    things you are interested in learning. Pro bono or
    volunteer work for a community organization may
    offer new opportunities, and your company may even
    support your time as a volunteer if you present it in a
    way that connects to current objectives.

2. **An internal "attagirl" or "attaboy."** It's okay to
    pat yourself on the back! Notice when you are doing
    well, and encourage yourself to keep going. Support
    yourself when you move in the direction of your
    aspirations.

3. **Create a "smile file."** Keep a file or drawer filled with
    notes of appreciation from clients, cartoons you like,
    greeting cards with meaningful wishes, and other
    items that make you feel good. Just like a shot of
    caffeine can wake up your energy, five minutes with
    your feel-good file can lift your spirits.

For Appreciating Others

1. **Acknowledge and thank them using details:** Show
    you're paying attention by being specific when you
    talk about results, methods, efforts, or obstacles
    they've overcome.

2. **Care about the causes they care about.** What chari-
    table organizations do they support? Is there an issue
    in their neighborhood they are worried about? Are
    they on a crusade about recycling? Do they donate

time to the Girl Scouts or a crisis hotline? Matching donations or volunteering when they do will create lasting memories.

3. **Relieve them of a burden.** If someone is deserving of appreciation, what can you do to make their work life easier or less stressful? If you don't know, ask!

4. **Your presence.** Showing up at someone's office to surprise them with a quick verbal thank-you and some focused attention can help set a great tone for their day. Taking a walk with them to give you both some fresh air, time to decompress, and a bit of movement can be a welcome break that will lift energy levels.

Use any or all of these methods to leverage the natural and powerful human tendency to appreciate being appreciated. Become a master at appreciating your own efforts and enjoying the boost of positive results it creates within you. By skillfully shifting from feeling resentful and neglected into the growth of more effective methods for orchestrating recognition, we can create benefits that extend far and wide.

WHY Do the Reflection Exercises?

» To increase your ability to appreciate yourself.

» So you can find more methods to express appreciation.

» To have more impact on others through appreciation.

» To create enthusiasm in yourself and those around you.

REFLECTION EXERCISES

1. When was the last time you were recognized at your job?

2. What immediate feelings did you have when this happened?

3. Notice your relationship to recognition from others. Do you have positive, negative, or ambivalent associations with being appreciated on the job?

4. In what ways do you show appreciation for yourself? Make a list of twelve ways you could appreciate a job you've done well. What kind of appreciation would meeting a long-term goal warrant? How about a smaller treat for the everyday triumphs?

5. Start tracking your experiments. Start a quick spreadsheet on appreciations with five columns (or draw one onto a page in your journal). Record:

   » **When:** Note the date and time.

   » **Who:** Name the individual or group you appreciated.

   » **Why:** Briefly state what they did that you appreciated.

   » **What:** Identify the type of appreciation: card, email, verbal recognition during a meeting, individual conversation, a gift, a coffee/lunch out, etc.

   » **Impact:** What result or reaction did you notice?

6. **Create your own menu.** Consider your favorite ways to renew, reset, or take care of yourself during your week (personally as well as professionally). What lifts your spirits? As something occurs to you, write it down. Keep this list in a place you can see as you work (like in a drawer you use often).

   When your personal resource level is low, choose an item from your menu and do it. When you are particularly proud of something you have accomplished, plan something from your menu to appreciate yourself. Include plenty of low-cost/low-effort items on your menu, such as calling a friend or taking a tea break with a colleague.

THE SHIFT:

—FROM—

"I'm not responsible for other
people's development"

—TOWARD—

"I can facilitate
an environment of growth
and improvement."

24

GROWING OTHERS

The passion for stretching yourself and sticking
to it, even (or especially) when it's not going well,
is the hallmark of the growth mindset. This is the
mindset that allows people to thrive during some
of the most challenging times in their lives.

—CAROL DWECK
Stanford professor and author of
Mindset: The New Psychology of Success

MY FIRST DEEP LESSON as a manager came in a canoe.

Starting up a summer preschool program at a family resort in
Wisconsin, I was joined by two bright, capable college students.
Since I had more experience with childcare centers, they put me
in charge, but these two gals were willing and eager to learn. I
tried to ensure that I had control of most of the decisions while I
mentored them, shared my knowledge, and gave them instructions
as we set up the programs, ordered supplies, discussed policies,
etc. We worked together for several weeks, and I thought things
were going swimmingly.

Then one day they suggested we take a morning off and head out on a canoe across the lake.

They paddled and I duffed. Looking back on it, that seemed symbolic—they were taking charge. Once we were out to the middle of the lake, they told me that they had learned a lot from me and were ready to take on more responsibility and ownership of their positions. Now that they had experienced multiple weeks of kids and understood our aims, they had ideas and approaches they wanted to try. Basically, in the nicest possible way, they were asking me to back off as a manager, lighten up, and treat them less like underlings. It felt like an affront to my leadership, yet it was really an opening for me to learn. Which would I choose? Would I be offended or choose the path of growth?

Protecting people from their own development is rarely, if ever, appreciated, let alone warranted. If people are willing to grow, good managers will find opportunities for them to do so.

The Most Important Job of a Manager

Protecting people from their own development is rarely, if ever, appreciated, let alone warranted. If people are willing to grow, good managers will find opportunities for them to do so. I was embarrassed about having overstepped my management role to a degree that these two gals needed to speak to me about it, but thank goodness they did. It was truly better for me to have partners in the success of the school than "helpers." We operated far more efficiently and got better at what we did each week over the rest of the summer.

I certainly could have been offended that they didn't appreciate "all I had done for them" or "respect my authority," but those lines of thought aren't helpful. Those are the types of thoughts that keep us stuck in the past and unproductive in growing to meet the future.

Giving responsibility and control to others, with support, creates a learning ground for all involved. This seems like it should be easy, but it takes courage, because things might get worse before they get better. For instance, have you ever watched a parent step in to take away a task just as their kid is experimenting and fumbling and learning how to do something? It's a little painful to watch the interaction, because the kid is being deprived of an opportunity to struggle and figure it out for herself. "Here, let me do it," you might hear the parent say. If you watch closely, you might also see the kid slump in resignation.

The same thing happens in the workplace. Being a "leader breeder" is an artful blend of letting go of the parts you once held tightly and grabbing on to the role of providing what others need to succeed—not what you need or what you want them to need. This is the managerial transition to sharing the responsibility for making decisions, trying out new approaches suggested by others, and allowing your team to take charge while they are still able to ask you questions and solicit your feedback. You become the safety net for their decisions as they take on the tasks for themselves. The decisions, progress, and success are theirs; the glow of setting them up for success is yours. As a team leader or manager, you learn how to

Our capacity to turn difficult situations into deep learning sets the stage for stretching into the development opportunities our workplace can offer.

observe their process and provide the support, encouragement, or instruction they need at the right time, adjusting things along the way.

The Developmental Workplace

As the world grows more complex, organizations want their workforce to be able to handle complexity and ambiguity, and to build the capacity to take on increasing levels of responsibility and challenge. This development has both a personal and professional component—growing up to see that our typical reaction isn't our only option can give way to greater choice and better navigation of the inner game of work. This results in improvements in outward job performance as well.

Harvard professor Robert Kegan explains that "when people do not have the capacity to meet the demands in their lives, they may feel unhappy, undervalued, and 'in over their heads.'"[25] Hard times can shrink rather than grow one's capacity, depending how the situation is interpreted and acted upon, as well as the degree of support available. Our capacity to turn difficult situations into deep learning sets the stage for stretching into the development opportunities our workplace can offer. As Jennifer Garvey Berger put it while writing about Kegan's ideas:

> A person's current developmental capacity is a kind of diversity that is so hidden that almost no one recognizes it. Recognized or not, though, developmental capacity affects everything a person is able to think or do.[26]

It takes perspective to look at our beliefs as something that can be examined, selected, and adjusted over time. Many of us confuse our first set of beliefs as a "truth" and experience a lack of adherence to them as not "being ourselves." We cling tightly to beliefs as if they are our identity. But who we are is much bigger than what we've known or believed from our past. How we make meaning in the world should evolve as we are able to understand the events of our lives differently through our growth. Again, as Berger described it, "New information may add to the *things* a person knows, but *trans*formation changes the *way* he or she knows those things."[27]

So what can you do to help your team members grow and develop while you are doing the same? There are many excellent resources on the keys to team success, such as psychological safety, transparency, trust, and more. Yet, applying those, or any other principles or efforts to make change with team members, follows the same A-W-S cycle we discussed in Part One.

AWARENESS

WILLINGNESS

SKILL

The Awareness-Willingness-Skill cycle is a simple and effective model for finding the development edge for our team members while supporting them to grow through their experiences. Within the system of organizational life, we are all connected. We can see that being a sponsor of our own and others' development is mutually reinforcing. Getting good at supporting and challenging others' growth is, in fact, supportive and challenging to our *own*.

Here is how the A-W-S model for both *horizontal* growth (the building of new, broader skillsets to accomplish more) and *vertical* growth (the inward building of higher levels of consciousness) can function through everyday work experiences.

Awareness

Recall a time when you had a professional growth spurt—a time when you were really learning a lot about your field, profession, or role. How did you first become aware of the areas in which you needed to "grow up"?

Becoming aware of the gaps between what we are bringing to the situation—our current capability—and what is required to succeed is the realization that kicks off deliberate growth on the job. Before we are aware, our developmental edge is in a blind spot—we don't know what we don't know. We are not choosing what to do about it, because we have no idea there is something that needs doing. Trying to help someone build skills before they are aware of the need to do so tends to be a waste of time. They just don't see the relevance and will fight to maintain the status quo—exactly the opposite of deliberate development.

On the other hand, you can help someone grow in awareness when you:

> » State the obvious in nonjudgmental ways: "You seem to be feeling stuck about what to do about such and such," or "I noticed fewer people speaking up after you expressed frustration in the last meeting."

> » Reflect on themes—using facts—from different occurrences. "Over the past month I noticed you seemed frustrated when x, y, and z happened. Is there something we need to discuss?"

> » Provide honest feedback with compassionate understanding. On the continuum from "blunt opinion" to "sugar coated," find an appropriate midpoint.

» Review team effectiveness assessments to uncover areas where you wish to grow and develop yourself as a leader or improve teamwork.

» Explore alternatives, such as, "Thinking back on that situation, are there any other ways it could have been handled better?" Just an awareness that there are other options in the face of any situation can help us see that we made a choice and can, in fact, choose differently.

Once they become aware of a potential for change, team members can receive your support to help them make change—that is, if they are *willing*.

Willingness

You may have noticed myriad ways people consciously and unconsciously resist change by blaming others, making excuses, and refusing to see how they are creating the challenges they face. This becomes particularly painful to watch when valued team members are damaging themselves, their reputation, or the organization's interests by their refusal to grow. Even if we are aware of a need to develop in a certain area, willingness is also a critical ingredient to getting better at what we do—and better at connecting it to who we are. As one of my colleagues likes to say, "They gotta wanna." Willingness is the pivotal factor that determines whether or not a person will move into deliberate practice.

As one of my colleagues likes to say, "They gotta wanna." Willingness is the pivotal factor that determines whether or not a person will move into deliberate practice.

To help team members build willingness, you can discuss the costs and benefits of the current behavior. Help them identify if there is resistance and what is causing concern. Make room to focus time and energy on the issue, even amid distractions. Encourage small, specific steps or thought experiments to explore new possibilities and develop other options. A lack of willingness can stem from seeing only the present circumstances and not believing that change is possible. Help them begin to identify the benefits: What could the future be like if they made a change? Whether we become willing because of a cost we want to avoid or a gain we want to acquire, it is only after we are willing that we begin paying attention to getting better and begin the process of building new *skills*.

Skill

Skill building is where the action is. This is where we *verb*. We read, discuss, try, study, experiment, ask, try again, fail, try something else, get slightly better, and then try again—more intelligently. It is an iterative process of developing skill and building new abilities in a specific area over time. Along the way, of course, you become *aware* of other areas that need development—and then launch into the cycle anew. We build the capability of growing ourselves and others as we develop new skills ourselves.

Growing Every Day

As we support and challenge the growth of team members by using everyday work experiences, it helps to notice opportunities for "spur-of-the-moment development." Here are six ways to help co-workers choose the path of growth in response to whatever comes their way:

1. **Give them developmental assignments:** Task the person with completing an assignment that is just a bit out of reach, and then be a thinking partner with them as they tackle it. This can spur tremendous, deliberate growth. This works well with practical skills such as planning, facilitating, organizing, and driving an initiative forward.

2. **Imagining a desired future:** Regarding any project or assignment, ask them what the ideal outcome would be or what success would look like for this situation. Help them build a robust picture of the future they are striving for.

3. **Facilitate straightforward discussions:** Create a culture of being honest about challenges and asking for and giving support. Share information about what is important and help team members understand how it may impact them.

4. **Nurture self-acceptance:** Encourage team members to allow themselves grace as they grow. Acknowledge the progress they have made, as well as areas for further development.

5. **Connect to the big picture:** The day-to-day grind is challenging. Look for opportunities to explore larger contexts.

6. **Insert some fun.** Look for humor and times to enjoy each other to give yourself and others a mental break and reward the hard work of growth.

7. **Walk the talk:** Discuss your own growth and development. Demonstrate the process of making change yourself to illustrate how it's done, and inspire others to join you. Keep your commitments to your own development objectives.

Conscious professionals make a practice of growing at work. Just like a meditation practice or practicing an athletic skill, they consistently return to where the path of growth leads next. As you focus on building the skills and capabilities to move forward, do so with a joyful heart, because this is truly work that matters—connecting with and living your values. Enjoy a deep sense of fulfillment as you master the complex and wonderful challenges ahead. Your enthusiasm for growth will be contagious!

WHY Do the Reflection Exercises?

» To improve your managerial skills.

» So you can support others in increasing their Third Paycheck.

» To engage those around you in learning while getting work done.

» To grow leadership potential in yourself and others as a constant practice.

REFLECTION EXERCISES

1. Consider a team member you work with. What do you appreciate about who he or she is? It's always a good idea to start with respect.

2. What do you know about what they enjoy about their work—their strengths and delights? And what they would consider their next level of achievement? What do they hope to do in the future? (If you don't know, once again, ask.)

3. Are they aware of their need to build skills? How do they think about their work quality?

4. What would you expect to see them do to build their skills, if they were willing?

5. What are their interests? Where would they go, what would they read, and/or how could they learn more in that area?

6. What can you do to encourage them to move forward on their skill building and to stick with it when the going gets rough?

If we don't change, we don't grow. If we don't grow, we are not really living. Growth demands a temporary surrender of security. It may mean a giving up of familiar but limiting patterns, safe but unrewarding work, values no longer believed in, relationships that have lost their meaning.

—GAIL SHEEHY
author and lecturer

GRATITUDE AND GRACE FOR THE JOURNEY

The leader for today and the future
will be focused on how to *be*—how to develop
quality, character, mindset, values,
principles, and courage.

—FRANCES HESSELBEIN

THAT MOMENT WHEN YOU feel at home with yourself—when major threats are distant or unlikely, and you aren't *too* worried about something you did or didn't do—is rare for most professionals. Living a full life with family and community while deeply caring about your work creates very little free time. There are so many loose ends, so many plans, hopes, and things we want to make better. It's part of our Developmental Drive. We are called, pushed, and drawn in so many directions. It can become a constant state of pushing on to the next destination rather than being present with the impact of the moment.

Feeling gratitude for what we have and where we are, instead of what we lack or where we need to go next, is a shift in perspective. I'm confident you're getting good at making shifts by now. Consciously choosing how you want to relate to a situation is a level of self-mastery that allows you to shape and reshape your experience, whatever comes your way. Building this type of mental agility improves almost everything in life. And it puts you in a position to choose, to change, to refine, and to fine-tune the song you wish to live and the ways you choose to serve, love, and enjoy the experience. Gratitude is both a choice and an outcome.

When I was a young manager, one of my employees gave me a perspective I've invoked many times since. As an introvert, she was tired of me asking the team spur-of-the-moment questions like, "What did you think?" about important issues. She wanted time to consider her opinions before sharing her thoughts. She wanted to contribute something of value and needed space to contemplate before responding. One meeting, she blurted out with irritation, "I can't really answer that. If you want to know what we think, you have to *give . . . us . . . time . . . to . . . think.*"

We need to set aside time to get in touch with our thoughts, feelings, intuition, and intentions if we are serious about bringing forth our best into the world.

Lightbulb!

Reflection is the backbone of this book's teachings. It's not so much "how to" as it is "how you discover." That's how self-directed development works. *Of course,* we need to set aside time to get in touch with our thoughts, feelings, intuition, and intentions if we are serious about bringing forth our best into the world. I hope these chapters have given you impetus, tools, and space to begin doing just that—transforming your life at work.

Being an extroverted, fast-moving sort myself, I always considered sitting still a waste of time. Then I heard Dr. Martin Luther King Jr.'s words, "I have so much to do today; I'll have to spend another half an hour on my knees." It took a long time for me to understand what he meant.

It took longer still for me to make the space for grace. Who knows how the universe really operates? All its mystery and wonder, from the tiniest particles to the vastness of the galaxies beyond our own, give me confidence that there is much we don't know. Considering that, how could it not be helpful to calm our mind and heart and focus on our deepest connection, intelligence, and insights to help us lead the way forward more consciously and capably?

Let me leave you with these intentions as you continue on your journey of becoming an evermore-conscious professional:

May your work grow you on the inside.

May you grow others by example.

May your family, community, and causes benefit from your new capabilities as a professional and a person.

May you bring who you are to what you do, so you can shape and grow the workplace.

May you have more awareness, willingness, and skill to apply in the areas where it matters most.

"I aim to put the most

powerful leadership methods

in the hands and hearts

of change makers, moving us

forward to a future

that is better for us all—

inside and out."

ABOUT THE AUTHOR

 **Jessica Hartung** has a passion for inspiring and equipping people to grow from their work to improve their lives. In 1998, she founded Integrated Work, a consulting firm that brings top-notch professional development to mission-driven leaders while being a learning laboratory for innovative work practices. Integrated Work focuses exclusively on growing mission-driven leaders personally, professionally, and collectively, using an integrated, heartfelt blend that elevates work experiences into the training ground for change-making leadership.

A sought-after coach, advisor, and facilitator, Jessica's secret sauce is using actual, real-life work challenges as case studies to grow new levels of leadership, personal success, and capability to dream more vividly and achieve more artfully. Now, she is working to make the same top-tier professional development that organizational clients enjoy available to all who seek it. Building ethical leadership at all levels, is how we advance humanity, protect our planet, and build a connected, compassionate, and educated society.

Jessica is an author for *Conscious Company* magazine and a coach for Emerging Women, as well as the Frances Hesselbein Global Student Leadership Summit.

To keep herself energized, Jessica gardens, volunteers, and reads voraciously. Jessica resides in Boulder, Colorado, with her husband, astrophysicist Stephen F. Hartung, and their two children.

NOTES

1. http://www.arthurashe.org. He founded the Arthur Ashe Foundation for the Defeat of AIDS and the Arthur Ashe Institute for Urban Health.

2. Frances Hesselbein is a highly respected expert in the field of contemporary leadership development. She is the founding president and CEO of The Frances Hesselbein Leadership Institute (now the Frances Hesselbein Leadership Forum), originally founded as The Peter F. Drucker Foundation for Nonprofit Management. She holds twenty-three honorary doctoral degrees, the Presidential Medal of Freedom, and many other awards recognizing her contributions to the field of service-oriented leadership.

3. Available on YouTube at: https://www.youtube.com/watch?v=J-swZaKN2Ic. (Or just search "The Power of Yet Carol Dweck" on YouTube.)

4. Ibid.

5. Bill J. Bonnstetter and Judy Suiter, *The Universal Language DISC: A Reverence Manual* (Scotsdale, AZ: Target Training International, 2004).

6. Robert Kegan and Lisa Laskow Lahey, *Immunity to Change: How to Overcome It and Unlock the Potential in Yourself and Your Organization* (Cambridge, MA: Harvard Business Review Press, 2009).

7. David Boud, Rosemary Keogh, and David Walker (ed.), *Reflection: Turning Experience into Learning* (New York: Nichols Publishing Company, 1985), 34.

8. Carmen Nobel, "Reflecting on Work Improves Job Performance," *Harvard Business School* (May 5, 2014), accessed: June 6, 2017, http://hbswk.hbs.edu/item/reflecting-on-work-improves-job-performance.

9. Ibid.

10. Science is clear about the link between writing and memory. Study after study shows you remember things better when you write them down. Neuropsychologists have identified the "generation" effect which describes that people have a better memory for material they themselves have generated versus material that has been read or watched. (Pam A. Mueller and Daniel M. Oppenheimer, "The Pen Is Mightier Than the Keyboard: Advantages of Longhand Over Laptop Note Taking," Psychological Science 25, no. 6 (April 23, 2014): https://doi.org/10.1177/0956797614524581.)

11. Ronald Heifetz, *Leadership without Easy Answers* (Cambridge, MA: Harvard University Press, 1998), 252-253.

12. The Arbinger Institute, *The Outward Mindset: Seeing Beyond Ourselves* (Oakland, CA: Berrett-Koehler Publishers, Inc., 2016). (I highly recommend this book to explore this concept further.)

13. Randall MacLowry (writer and director), "*Silicon Valley* tells the story of the scientists who transformed a rural southern California county into a hub of technology innovation," *American Experience*, season 25, episode 5, video.

14. Meena Thuraisingham, *Careers Unplugged: Essential Choices for a Great Career* (Singapore: Bluetoffee Pte Ltd., 2007), 141.

15. Adam Grant, *Give and Take: A Revolutionary Approach to Success* (New York: Viking, 2013), and Adam Grant, "Are You a Giver or a Taker?: A Revolutionary Approach to Success," TED Talk, November 2016, https://www.ted.com/talks/adam_grant_are_you_a_giver_or_a_taker.

16. Amy C. Edmondson, *Teaming: How Organizations Learn, Innovate, and Compete in the Knowledge Economy* (Hoboken, NJ: John Wiley & Sons, Inc., 2012). Search her on YouTube for videos of her presentations.

17. Annie McKee, "Being Happy at Work Matters," *Harvard Business Review* (November 14, 2014), accessed March 19, 2018, https://hbr.org/2014/11/being-happy-at-work-matters; Karlyn Borysenko, "The Business Benefits of Happy Employees," *Talent Management and HR* (September 16, 2016), accessed March 19, 2018, https://www.tlnt.com/the-business-benefits-of-happy-employees/; and Jonha Revesencio, "Why Happy Employees Are 12% More Productive," *Fast Company* (July 22, 2015), accessed March 19, 2018, https://www.fastcompany.com/3048751/happy-employees-are-12-more-productive-at-work.

18. Steven Pressfield, *The War of Art: Break Through the Blocks and Win Your Inner Creative Battles* (New York: Warner Books, 2003), xvii, 40.

19. Aaron Hurst, *The Purpose Economy: How Your Desire for Impact, Personal Growth, and Community Is Changing the World* (Boise, Idaho: Elevate Publishing, 2016), 3, 26.

20. Morten T. Hansen, "How to Succeed in Business? Do Less," *Wall Street Journal*, January 12, 2018, https://www.wsj.com/articles/how-to-succeed-in-business-do-less-1515770816.

21. http://www.bostonglobe.com/metro/2013/09/27/malala-yousafzai-pakistani-teen-shot-taliban-tells-harvard-audience-that-education-right-for-all/6cZBanOM4J3cAnmRZLfUmI/story.html.

22. Roger Fisher and William Ury, *Getting to Yes: Negotiating Agreement Without Giving In* (New York: Penguin Books, 1991), 97-106.

23. Tom Rath and Donald O. Clifton, *How Full Is Your Bucket? Positive Strategies for Work and Life* (New York: Gallup Press, 2001), 27.

24. *Merriam-Webster*, s.v. "appreciate," last modified February 1, 2018, https://www.merriam-webster.com/dictionary/appreciate.

25. Jennifer Garvey Berger, "A summary of the Constructive-Developmental Theory of Robert Kegan," accessed October 24, 2018, https://www.coursehero.com/file/20070928/berger-on-kegan-narrative-1/.

26. Ibid.

27. Ibid.

TAKE A DEEPER DIVE INTO YOUR GROWTH AS A
CONSCIOUS PROFESSIONAL

THE CONSCIOUS PROFESSIONAL is packed with tools and strategies based on the real-world experience of growing leadership on the job. It has so much to offer that some find it difficult to know where to begin putting all its wisdom into action. That is why Jessica has created *The Conscious Professional Workbook*. This workbook guides you through some key processes for transforming your life at work. You will see results as you use the exercises and apply them personally and professionally. You can grow in place without needing anyone else's permission, support, or endorsement.

THE CONSCIOUS PROFESSIONAL WORKBOOK
GET IT NOW TO ENJOY THESE BENEFITS:

» Know that you are Conscious Professional who has the power to transform your life at work.

» Gain confidence from consistent practice, new skills, and the courage to experiment at your developmental edges.

» Take ownership of a growth mindset and know you are a deliberately developmental individual.

» Watch yourself make micro-identity shifts as you grow and develop. Know you have the power to change how you see yourself.

» Take control of your professional development by successfully running action learning experiments where you decide.

» Transform pain, fear, and doubt to make these emotions your allies. Turn them into teachers at work and beyond.

» Gain greater peace by knowing where in the Awareness - Willingness - Skill cycle you currently are on multiple issues.

» Increase your ability to influence the organization you work with, positively affect team dynamics, and help transform the lives of others at work as well.

» Finding greater peace as you clarify your focus, find a greater sense of purpose, and determine what you stand for.

Sign up now at: CONSCIOUSPROFESSIONAL.COM/WORKBOOK

SUPPLEMENT YOUR GROWTH WITH MORE FROM THE
CONSCIOUS PROFESSIONAL

TO DOWNLOAD Jessica's press kit and discover other companion products from Jessica for your journey, visit:

CONSCIOUSPROFESSIONAL.COM

TO PLACE BULK ORDERS for you team or organization (*comes with a free Book Club Guide!*), download Jessica's press kit and discover other companion products from Jessica for your journey, head over to:

CONSCIOUSPROFESSIONAL.COM/BOOK-CLUB

TO ACCESS your free worksheets to supplement the tools described in this book, visit:

CONSCIOUSPROFESSIONAL.COM/WORKSHEETS

THE CONSCIOUS PROFESSIONAL'S goal is to inspire shifts in your experience at work and in life. Part of the process the book takes its readers through is in the reflection questions at the end of each chapter. Reflection is the Miracle-Gro® of professional and personal development! To allow you more space to answer these reflection questions for yourself, and for additional reflections to support you in deepening your understanding in the growth process, Jessica is designing a Conscious Professional companion journal. To be notified of the journal's release date, please sign up at:

CONSCIOUSPROFESSIONAL.COM/JOURNAL

JOIN THE
CONSCIOUS
PROFESSIONAL
COMMUNITY!

TO STAY UP TO DATE with the author and engage in community discussion around professional development topics, visit:

JESSICA**HARTUNG**.COM

...and follow the Conscious Professional blog. Here Jessica is sharing her most recent thoughts and actions that you may find useful on your journey.

Jessica delivers keynote speaking engagements, corporate conference appearances, workshops, as well as podcast interviews. You can find topics for speaking engagements and workshops on the main page. One-on-one coaching and intensive short term video coaching is available for those looking for personal application of the work. Please visit the contact page to get in touch!

Jessica Hartung
Purpose – Growth – Connection